SIMPLY HOME

DECORATING

Melissa Michaels

TEN PEAKS PRESS®
EUGENE, OR

Published in association with William K. Jensen Literary Agency,
119 Bampton Court, Eugene, Oregon 97404

Cover and interior design by Faceout Studio

For bulk or special sales, please call 1-800-547-8979.
Email: Customerservice@hhpbooks.com

 TEN PEAKS PRESS is a federally registered trademark of The Hawkins Children's LLC.
Harvest House Publishers, Inc., is the exclusive licensee of this trademark.

SIMPLY HOME

Copyright © 2017, 2018 by Melissa Michaels
Published by Ten Peaks Press, an imprint of Harvest House Publishers
Eugene, Oregon 97408

ISBN 978-0-7369-8767-7 (hardcover)
Library of Congress Control Number: 2022952321

Previously published as *Simple Decorating* and *Simple Organizing* by Melissa Michaels

Printed in China

23 24 25 26 27 28 29 30 31 / RDS / 10 9 8 7 6 5 4 3 2 1

Contents

A PLACE YOU CAN CALL HOME 8

SIGNATURE STYLE 9

MEMORABLE MOOD 21

BEAUTIFUL BACKDROPS 37

SIMPLIFIED SPACES 51

CREATIVE CONCEALMENTS 67

TOUCHABLE TEXTURES 81

ARTFUL ACCESSORIES 95

SIMPLE DECORATING

is for real life—including the chaos of change. This book features images of our own homes in various seasons as well as through moves from one home to another. You will see how we used accessories and furniture in different ways and settings over the years. So, welcome to these imperfect and real spaces! They offer practical tips and decorating lessons learned over time. As you consider ideas for your home, remember that imperfection doesn't have to feel like a limitation—it can be a creative opportunity to make the most of what you have and love.

A PLACE YOU
CAN CALL HOME

Do you ever find yourself in a decorating slump or just plain ol' STUCK? Whether you spend hours drooling over your favorite rooms on Pinterest or feel so frozen you don't even know what to look for, I created this little guide to give you a gentle nudge toward a home you'll love.

Feeling confident in your own style and with your decor choices might take time. It helps to start with the courage to experiment and the inspiration to spark your ideas. If you don't know your style or the mood you're after, you can end up with a hodgepodge of items that individually seemed like good ideas but altogether just don't work. You might have hand-me-downs to sit on, an empty space still waiting for inspiration, or a room full of pieces you love. No matter what your starting point is, if you know how to mix and match elements together, you can make your unique design statement and a home that is exactly how you dream it should be.

The truth I share every day on *The Inspired Room* blog and will express in these pages is that you don't have to start with a dreamy house, nor do you have to spend a fortune to make what you have more beautiful. A magazine or Internet image of a room that catches your eye is often a Photoshop-enhanced presentation of a well-designed corner with curated items all set up for the perfect shot. While a beautiful photo can inspire us and we might even capture magazine cover looks, what really matters in our home is how it feels to be there. A home is a place to dwell. It's a sanctuary that can invite us to be ourselves. Our home should be a comfortable haven, with rooms and spaces we enjoy being in.

Every part of your home can be an authentic reflection of what you love, arranged in a livable, pleasing, and lovable space for your family to gather. So let's explore how you can simply create a beautiful place that you can call home in every sense of the word.

Feeling confident in your own style
and with your decor choices might take time.
It helps to start with the courage to experiment
and the inspiration to spark your ideas.

Signature
STYLE

Signature
STYLE

If you pick up a design book or magazine, you will often find that each one represents a specific style, with tips and photo illustrations for how to achieve that look. You may even find quizzes to identify your style or definitions of various looks to choose from. Yet a home is so personal!

While it can be helpful to have terms to describe your signature look, I don't think you actually have to *choose* a style, especially one that has its own label in a book or in the design world. In fact, to have a truly personal style, there has to be something a bit unexpected about it. Something previously undefined. Something that is all you.

You will define your style by *living* it first. Your life experiences and personal preferences should inspire the look and feel of your home. Perhaps like me, your faith and family are priorities. What motivates your decisions, and what passions impact your life? These are elements you can incorporate into your home. No one will share your exact style because there is only one you! Your style will ebb and flow through each changing season of your life, springing from your unique personality and reflecting the joy you find in living. So go ahead and create a style that has no official designer name. Boldly design a look inspired by your life and everything you love. Mix it all up to give your home its own unique flair, creating the perfect space for you to come home to each day!

1 | DESIGN YOUR LIFE FIRST

Make style and decor choices that support the life you have and the one you want. If you have pets or small children, you might pay more attention to the durability of fabrics. If you can't spend much time keeping up your home, make decor choices that are simpler and more forgiving so you can spend less time cleaning. If you hope to travel more, go for low-maintenance options. Your home is *for* you and your family, so always consider how your home can accommodate what you enjoy. A comfortable place to watch movies? Space to cook a delicious meal? An organized craft closet to inspire your hobbies?

Consider the unique personality and needs of you and your family. Do you need an escape, a retreat from busy or stressful days at work? Do you want your home to be a place for community with an open door and gathering spaces for neighbors and friends? Make choices that will shape your home into a place where you get to be yourself.

Think about future goals and needs. In light of where you're headed, is your home a short-term or life-long dwelling? If you will move again in the near future, keep affordability, mobility, and flexibility in mind as you select furniture and styles, while still creating a place you feel comfortable in for the time being. If you are settling in for the long term, what choices might grow with you and your family's needs? What areas of improvement might you invest in more fully?

2 | DISCOVER YOUR STYLE

What do you love? What says "home" when you walk into a room? Discover your style by noticing what tones, colors, shapes, and arrangements you would like your home to model in its own way—in your own way. Descriptive words and inspirational images will help lead the way!

Brainstorm inspiration words. Create a short list of words to express the look you want. Think about who you are, what you like, and how others might describe you. Consider the style of your home's architecture, the surrounding landscape, your favorite books, hobbies, style of clothing, etc. If you don't live alone, list words that describe your family, your spouse. A few of my inspiration words are:

nature, clean	happy, sophisticated	collected, refreshing
airy, light	approachable, relaxed	sea, getaway

Browse images. Consider it an investment and not an indulgence to look at magazines and favorite online sources for photos of rooms you connect with. If you see a style you love, study it and dream up your version of it. The most helpful examples will have at least one aspect in common with your space: room size or layout, style of windows, architectural details, etc. This might spark more ideas for your inspiration word list.

3

DIY: CRAFT AN INSPIRATION BOARD

Keep your style in mind and in view with an inspiration board for your home or for each room! You can make a virtual one, but consider creating at least one physical board as an exercise in bringing your style to life.

1. Choose a bulletin board. Or find a blank space on a wall you can take over for a season.

2. Gather some inspiration elements. Search your home, magazines, online sources, and even the outdoors for photos or objects that represent what makes your heart sing. Include mementos, scrapbook paper, fabric and paint swatches, fonts, photos, leaves or flowers, and your doodles of lamps, patterns, or furniture arrangements.

3. Arrange and pin the pieces. The pleasure of grouping, overlapping, and rearranging the colors, photos, textures, and ideas becomes a vacation from your usual routine. It can be addicting!

4. Hang the board where it will motivate you. But don't stop there. Continue brainstorming throughout the week. Pull elements down that you grow tired of and put new ones up as you feel inspired. See what works, what clashes, what feeds your vision!

5. Take a photo. This visual reference will keep you focused on your style goals when you are out looking for particular pieces.

4 | CREATE A STYLE WISH LIST

If you have a specific style you like, it's helpful to discover which elements will inspire your own look. Let's say you want a farmhouse-style home. Do some research of designers online or in books to find others who have a similar aesthetic. Dissect their rooms and make a list of elements used in their designs that you could incorporate into your own. Don't be intimidated by price tags or designer brands. Look closely at your favorite designers' rooms, and you'll likely find you can get a similar look for less. Keep your style wish list on hand for when you shop! Your list will help you to have specific pursuits at retail outlets, estate sales, or thrift stores and confirm what you need to weed out.

Include in your list both general references (more antiques, certain colors) and specific elements (iron chandelier, wood trestle table). Once you can translate your style into tangibles, you'll be able to reduce costly and often regrettable random purchases.

5 | CHANGE YOUR STYLE ON A BUDGET

When you think a room feels uninspired and you're tight on funds, consider it an opportunity to be more creative. What can you do for free (or cheap)?

Try something unexpected. Use a stool for an end table, floor pillows for casual extra seating, a hutch as a bookcase, or a wire basket as wall art.

Clear out the unloved. Identify things you don't want or need. You might find stuff tucked away that you could repurpose or sell to save up for something you do want!

Get sentimental. Dig through your postcards and greeting cards. Hang some special notes or current family memories with pushpins or frames.

Look at the overlooked. Missed decorating opportunities are plentiful. Restyle the top of your dresser or end table. What needs to be dealt with, hung up, or put away?

Shake things up. Which items could you move to a new spot? Your usual nightstand lamp could add a homey touch to your kitchen counter. Your wall art in the entry might look wonderful above your bed!

6

MIX AND MATCH TO GET YOUR LOOK

Style mixing can be a challenging art form. Nobody wants a living room that looks like a yard sale explosion, but staying safe with a matchy-matchy look won't help you shape your signature style. There are ways to mix and match and still have harmony.

SURPRISE

If you have a basic look you are going for, whether that be a particular era or style or basic color scheme, throw in a twist with a piece that doesn't fit the rule so it can stand out as fresh.

SIMPLIFY

When mixing styles, reduce excess clutter that can steal the show and add confusion. Remove unnecessary items off your mantel and tables. Also, simple, neutral wall colors will allow your variety of furniture and accessories to be the focus.

UNITE

A vibrant color on one focal piece brings a pop of personality to a space and creates a visual center. Or one color repeated at least three times in a room (throw pillows, blankets, painted furniture, accessories, and wall colors) can bring a cohesive look to eclectic furniture.

CELEBRATE

Don't force your signature style to fit one label. As long as you can identify it when you see it, feel it, or spot the ideal complement to it, celebrate *your* style.

7 | LET YOUR STORY AND HOME EVOLVE

Creating your home is like writing an ongoing love story. It will keep evolving just as your life and family will. Even though you might be impatient for the end result, remember that the creation process is part of the joy.

+ Use what you have as a starting place and then add one layer at a time.

+ Balance seasons of making changes with seasons of savoring and waiting.

+ Believe that "good enough" really *is* good enough for now.

+ Look for creative solutions, not expensive ones.

+ Let go of a look you used to love in order to make room for your next chapter.

Love your space even during the in-between stage. Let's face it. That stage can be all the time. But that's okay. It's your home, not a showroom. Taking time to hunt for the right pieces and shape your style will ultimately create a more interesting story.

The creation process is part of the joy.

Memorable
MOOD

Memorable
MOOD

If you were to pick your favorite escape, the place you'd go to feel refreshed, more fully alive, and in touch with what you most love, where would you go? Close your eyes and picture yourself heading there right now. Perhaps you would head to a local coffeehouse or travel to a charming seaside inn. Maybe your mind travels through time to a place you used to love.

So often the highlight of the year is our vacation, the time we leave our home to go to a different place to rest and rejuvenate. Those getaways from everyday stress and routine are important, but our home is where we spend most of our time. It should be the place that nurtures us and enhances our life, perhaps as much or more than any other place on earth. With some attention to detail and a few extra touches, we can create the mood we long for right where we eat, sleep, live life, and daydream.

You see, the real secret to creating a beautiful space isn't found in just buying the right things or even in having a perfect house to begin with. It's in knowing how to create a place that evokes a feeling. Your home can spark happiness and comfort, joy and peace—whatever you envision as the perfect mood for your escape from the world right there in your own sanctuary.

8 | DRAW INSPIRATION FROM YOUR FAVORITE PLACES

Look to your favorite places to find design elements you can incorporate to create the same mood for your home. When you translate the mood of a special place into ambience for your home, it takes on a richly personal feel.

SPECIAL PLACE	DESIGN POSSIBILITIES
A charming cafe	White walls, marble-and-wood bistro table, chalkboard on the wall
Spas or salons	Dim lighting, natural elements, soothing music
A favorite boutique	Floral wallpaper, crystal chandelier, gold mirrors
A dream island vacation	Coastal elements, lots of natural light, sea-inspired colors
Library nooks	Tall bookshelves, stacks of hardback books, leather chairs
Botanical gardens	Potted plants, nature-inspired colors, botanical prints
European destinations	Antiques, architectural elements, paintings of European settings

9 | SET THE MOOD FOR YOUR SENSES

Engaged senses create and awaken good memories, inspire contentment, and transform your surroundings and your mood. Give your senses something to celebrate.

SIGHT

What makes your eyes light up? Create a visual feast that nourishes your sense of home with:

+ furnishings and accessories in different sizes, shapes, and visual weight

+ vibrant, patterned areas balanced with simplicity so your eyes have a place to rest

+ wall colors that flow room to room for visual expansion

+ textures, colors, patterns, shapes, light, and shadow that together create a pleasing big picture

TOUCH

Pay attention to textures as you make decorating decisions and collect:

+ fabrics, accessories, floor coverings, counter materials, or furnishings

+ paired opposites—rough with smooth, shiny with dull, woven with silky

+ natural elements, including wood, stone, and plants for dimension

+ soft additions, such as down-filled pillows, lush blankets, thick natural fiber rugs

+ irresistible touches, such as luxurious sheets, fluffy towels, glass bowls in the kitchen

SMELL

Make a lasting and good impression on guests and your family with a nice scent and a clean home:

+ flower arrangements with subtle scents infuse bedrooms, entries, and bathrooms with beauty

+ signature scents created with candles and natural elements—such as vanilla and nutmeg, cloves for cozy moods, and lemon, jasmine, and orange for vibrant ones—help set a pleasing mood

+ unscented home cleansers will invite even sensitive noses to take deep, happy breaths

SOUND

Create a personalized soundtrack for your family's life with:

+ motivating and mood-setting music for different times of day and activities, such as housework or a dinner party.

+ limited contrasting sounds or repetitious phone beeps and alerts that can agitate

+ access to gentle outside sounds, such as the wind, water features, birds

+ silence during segments of the day

TASTE

Good taste is not just about style, but also about creating home spaces to experience the sense of taste. Try:

+ a soothing area to brew your morning coffee or tea for a day-making ritual

+ food prep stations and dining spaces that suit your style and invite others to savor and stay

+ organized pantries, cupboards, and refrigerators that set the stage to experience good food

HUMOR

Don't leave out your sense of humor! Laughter is always on my family's soundtrack. When a style touch represents our version of comedy, all the better. I'm never opposed to adding a few quirky animals here and there on anything from fabric to accessories in my home! Consider how you might bring your sense of humor to the spirit of your sanctuary.

10 | DISCOVER 8 WAYS TO A HAPPY HOME

1. **Fall in love with one corner.** If your home seems as if it's falling apart, create one happy corner in your study, dining room, or bedroom.

2. **Go back to basic routines.** As you do laundry, cook, or empty the dishwasher, think about how you are improving your home and state of mind. Tidy, putter, relax. Remind yourself of the simple routines, habits, and rhythms that give you peace.

3. **Let home be the centerpiece of your joy.** What are 20 things you look forward to doing in your home? Sort books, create a new display of accessories, rearrange furniture, and place inspiring quotes and photos of people you love around your home. Being optimistic today ensures more joy tomorrow.

4. **Reset the day.** Step away from a stressful house project to change your disposition. Take a walk, sip coffee on the porch, or window-shop to reset the day toward happiness.

5. **Dream.** Imagine the things you would do to your home if time or money were unlimited. Then decide how to make one of those dreams come true soon with a little creativity.

6. **Count those blessings.** Thankfulness for the home you have is an important part of loving life. If you are frustrated by a lack of progress, count the things you love about your home as is.

7. **Treat yourself.** What would make you happy right now? A new pillow in your reading nook chair? A fresh doormat? Pretty, plush towels? A woven basket for your mail? Simple treats can make a big difference in your mood, motivation, and creativity.

8. **Share your home.** Invite friends over to enjoy a space you recently saved from clutter. Gather neighbors on your porch for an impromptu dessert. Hospitality, laughter, and shared moments will remind you of all that makes you happy.

11 | TAKE YOUR CUES FROM THE SEASONS

Even if your corner of the world doesn't show the seasons, create the impression of seasonal freshness and ambience with simple changes around the house.

Enjoy the bounty of the season. Fresh and seasonal fruits and vegetables break up the monotony in your diet and in the colors and shapes you bring into your home. Don't forget to infuse your home with the scents of the season.

Inspire thanksgiving all year. Set a gratitude journal in the entry or living room and invite family and friends to add to it each season.

Capture seasonal scenes. During different times of the year, take photos of your yard, local park, or favorite downtown street. Frame those photos and incorporate them into your decor. Set a summer image by your nightstand when winter stretches on too long.

Keep decorations simple. A seasonal wreath on the front door, a basket of apples on the counter, or a bouquet of freesia can be enough to make a statement.

12 | INSPIRE THE ATMOSPHERE YOU WANT

LIVELY

Your home is where you can come alive and delight in the details. Create an energizing space to boost your mood with just the right mix of elements to inspire and recharge the life you want to live with:

graphic fabric patterns

splashes of vibrant hues

contrasting colors

strikingly shaped accessories

mixed styles of furnishings

bold artwork

displayed collections

energizing music

furniture for people to gather

fresh floral arrangements

dramatic focal points

quirky statement pieces

LOVE

is patient
is kind
does not envy
does not boast
is not proud
does not dishonor others
is not self seeking
is not easily angered
keeps no record of wrongs
does not delight in evil
rejoices with the truth
always protects
always trusts
always hopes
always perseveres

1 Corinthians 13:4-7

SERENE

Do you crave an escape from the noise and frantic pace of the outside world? The choices you make can set a soothing ambience that quiets your mind and inspires rest and relaxation. Your home is where you can be refreshed with:

solid neutral fabrics	fewer pieces
restful colors	clearer surfaces
soft edges	more white space
organic elements	water features
subtle patterns	closed storage
less contrast	simplified design elements

13 | LIGHTEN UP

Your atmosphere will come together when the lighting does. Illuminate your favorite spaces!

+ Walk around your home and note the lights, lamps, dark corners, and the ambience. Then write down where you need lighting for mood, specific tasks, and personality.

+ Let natural daylight into your space with sheer curtains or adjustable shutters and blinds.

+ Use multiple light sources to soften dark corners and cozy up a room instantly.

+ Choose a larger lamp than you might normally consider or enjoy a new creative shape, color, or personality.

+ Add a smaller lamp or two on a console table for charm.

+ Bring in a floor lamp. I prefer small-scale, pharmacy-style metal lamps because they don't take up much room and still add light and personality.

+ Use the right lightbulb for the desired effect. Consider "warm light" bulbs for lamps and "daylight" bulbs for garages or other significant task areas.

+ Mix in two large lamps to enhance conversation areas.

+ Welcome people with gentle lighting in the entryway with wall lamps, sconces, or a small lamp on a table.

+ Consider sconces or the surprise touch of a lamp for ambient light in the kitchen.

+ In the bedroom, overhead lights don't inspire romance or rest, so select lamps that enhance visibility as well as tone, such as nightstand lamps or plug-in style wall sconces for reading.

+ Allow for mood flexibility with dimmer switches in any room!

+ Add special lighting for variety and delight with string lights, hurricane lamps, chandeliers, outdoor lighting features used inside, and candles and more candles.

+ Reflect and maximize light with well-placed mirrors and glass.

14 | LISTEN TO YOUR HOME

Do you ever feel limited by the style of your house, the furniture you've had a long time, or the current trend options? In your heart, you're sure your house would look best with a certain color scheme or style of furniture, but you find yourself stuck by how you think it's "supposed" to be. You might hesitate to try something new because you aren't sure if you can trust your instincts.

What you're sensing in your heart might actually be your house crying out for a fresher color scheme or simplified accessories. An older home might be wishing to retain her charm but with a little more spunk. Of course, a house doesn't literally speak, but consider how you feel in your space to determine what your house actually needs.

What is your house telling you? Try whatever your home is asking for. Worst outcome? You don't like it any better. But best case scenario? You love the new look.

Consider how you feel in your space to determine what your house actually needs.

Beautiful
BACKDROPS

Beautiful
BACKDROPS

Have you ever carefully arranged your furniture and still felt that your room wasn't quite right? Maybe you even piled on the accessories to try to fix it, but something was definitely missing. Or do you sometimes wonder if the best way to decorate a room is to just get a new sofa or perfect chairs? New furniture *is* always fun, but the real secret to creating a beautiful room isn't the right sofa or combination of accessories. It's the *shell* of the room that will make everything else shine!

When an Instagram or Pinterest photo of a beautiful room captures your attention, the backdrop is probably a big part of the attraction. Some of your favorite dream rooms might have charming details such as shiplap walls, endless wood floors, or big windows trimmed in substantial moldings with gorgeous sunlight streaming through.

How wonderful if you have those extra touches or are in a position to add them to your space. But even if real life includes dingy carpet, small windows, or lackluster rooms, there is still hope. There are plenty of simple ways to enhance the architectural impact and that all-important shell for even the humblest of rooms.

15 | CREATE VISUAL FLOW ROOM TO ROOM

Evaluate the visual connection between your spaces. Choose a spot in your home from which to look around 360 degrees. Is there a sense of flow in flooring, colors, furniture, and accents? What stands out in a good or bad way?

Remove objects of distraction. Identify and adjust anything that competes for visual attention. Simplifying your stuff gives your eyes places to rest and frees up the flow between rooms.

Plan your color choices. Select wall colors that offer pleasant contrasts or complements when viewed together. You can achieve a more subtle color flow between adjoining rooms by selecting the same paint for both spaces while adding white paint to lighten the effect in one of the rooms. (Test the ratio until you get a shade you like.) Or use subtly different tones from the same color palette.

Unite with an accent color. Lightly weave an accent color throughout the house in fabrics, curtains, rugs, ceramics, framed art, painted doors, and furniture.

16 | SET THE SCENE WITH PAINT

Walls are the largest backdrop in your home, and their color will make a big impact on the visual flow and the mood of each room. Here are some guides to help you choose perfect-for-you backdrops.

Choose your wall paint colors last. Ideally, let your decor choices evolve and then choose a paint color and finish that will complement rather that dictate your decisions. It's more enjoyable to select furniture you want and then find a complementary paint color than to shop for a sofa and rug based on a predetermined but potentially limiting paint color. You can also enhance and unite furniture and accessories you already have with a complementary backdrop.

Find inspiration for your colors. Look around at nature, books, rugs, paintings, fabrics, accessories, landscape tones...everywhere and anywhere. I usually begin with a color scheme that captures the general mood I want and reflects the surroundings outside and inside my home.

Make it easy. If you become overwhelmed by paint choices, go with a paint brand's recommended palette and then add your personality with slight adjustments or accent colors.

Consider neutrals. If you have good natural light, all white walls can be a great backdrop. Otherwise, the space can feel cold and lifeless. A soft neutral like greige or taupe can be a pleasing way to warm a room.

Don't be intimidated by a dark color. Whether you paint a full room or just one wall, a dark color adds dramatic contrast. Paired with light trim, it can be striking.

Soften harsh lines. If your home has awkward angles, all one tone on the walls, ceiling, and even trim can reduce the sharp lines.

Paint stripes. Bring visual depth and space to a room with stripes on one wall.

Test your choice. Before buying a gallon, paint a large sample section of the color on several walls and observe it for a couple days. The look of a color can change significantly depending on the light.

Make it fun. There are many clever options. Try chalkboard or dry-erase paint in an office, kids' rooms, the pantry (great for shopping lists), or on an interior door.

17 | DEFINE SPACE AND STYLE WITH RUGS

Rugs can make a perfect style statement. They tend to cover a large portion of a room, so selecting the right one for your space is important. With so many choices for sizes, patterns, and colors, these five guiding tips can be helpful.

1. Area rugs can be placed right over existing carpet, with or without a rug pad, to conceal less than ideal flooring, add style, increase comfort, or to help pull together a room.

2. Most rooms with conversation areas benefit from a rug at least 8' x 10' in size. A large room might need a bigger rug or more than one to define multiple functional areas of the space. A 4' x 6' or 5' x 7' can be perfect sizes in an entry or next to a bed.

3. When using a rug to define a space, choose one large enough that it at least fits under the front legs of each furniture piece. This unites the furniture and makes the room feel larger.

4. Runners can brighten up a dark hallway or be a perfect style statement in a kitchen. Be mindful of the rug patterns in adjoining spaces! If you choose a lively-patterned rug for your living room, select a solid, simple stripe or natural weave for an adjoining room or hallway. Too many rugs in a similar pattern or scale can compete for attention and overwhelm a space.

5. If you have neutral and solid upholstery in your space, a patterned rug can be the style setter you need to give your space the wow factor. If a room includes statement patterns and colorful pieces, consider selecting a rug that is textured—think sisal, jute, seagrass—or subtly patterned.

18 | MAXIMIZE YOUR WINDOWS

How you dress your windows can transform a room. Get creative as you consider which hanging preferences, treatment choices, and fabrics bring the best design layers to your home.

Hang curtains tall and wide. Your windows will appear much larger and more light will get in when you hang treatments above and beyond the window frame. I often hang my curtains almost to the ceiling, but only if it works in proportion to the space. If the area of blank wall above your window is too large, hanging the curtains high can dwarf the window.

Use lots of panels. Strive to add enough panels so the width of the fabric is at least double that of the window for fullness.

Place blinds above the window frame. If your window has no molding to interfere with the flow of a roll-up blind, consider attaching the top of the blind directly to the wall above for a graceful, elongated look.

BEFORE

Order blinds to fit. If you have oddly sized windows, order blinds to your specs. If your window is just quite large, you can hang multiple, narrower panels of blinds.

Show off molding with fixed, short rods. Avoid having a distracting line across pretty window molding by placing short, stationary rods only on either side of the window, rather than all the way across. The panels will soften the look while also highlighting the molding.

Add character and function with shutters. Adjustable shutters allow light in and limit visibility from outside, and they are so charming.

Do what works. In our old laundry room, I hung a curtain panel, rolled it up, and tied it in place with twine so it had the appearance of an adjustable shade with the ease of a simple solution.

AFTER

19 | SELECT CURTAINS FOR EFFECT

+ Heavier fabrics are attractive when they hang to the floor.

+ Lighter fabrics look lovely a bit longer than floor length so they "puddle" and create a soft cloud.

+ Curtains too short? Sew additional fabric onto the base of your curtains for a more dramatic length and hang.

+ A long, single panel might be all you need for a special small window. Draw the curtain panel back with a tie or an ornate rod for a touch of elegance in a bedroom.

20 | EMBELLISH WITH ARCHITECTURAL DETAILS

When it comes to architectural interest, it's all about the details. Think beyond basic builder style and add architectural touches to your home for extra charm and a sense of quality.

+ Add character with wainscoting, which also provides extra support for hooks and other hardware.

+ Install shiplap or tongue-and-groove paneling vertically or horizontally on walls (ceilings too) for a grand impression.

+ Use strips of molding to make current baseboards more substantial, to create your own crown molding at the ceiling line, and to enhance cupboard, cabinet, or room doors.

+ Place finials on your curtain rods for extra eye candy.

+ Upgrade hardware to transform spaces. Consider new door handles, drawer pulls, switch plates, or hooks.

+ Refresh tired cabinets by adhering a layer of veneer paneling, such as beadboard or strips of molding or even bamboo, to create dimension and personality.

+ Remove kitchen or hutch cupboard doors to create open shelving and a significant but easy "architectural" change.

21 | DIY: DESIGN A PERSONALIZED MAP WALL

The map wall I created attracted a lot of interest and questions on my blog, but I must confess that my first attempt was a big fail. Often the best personal touches to a home have a story behind them! I initially tried to put up the maps with wallpaper paste, which did not allow for me to adjust the pieces as I went. I ended up tearing them down and starting over...and finishing this easy way.

1. Select heavy sheets of wrapping paper. Choose maps that represent places you have traveled to, lands you hope to visit someday, or countries where your family originates from. Or select other patterns that inspire you! Make it a meaningful display.

2. Hang the paper with pushpins. Choose pins that suit your decor: regular pins or those with flat or decorative heads. Make sure they are sturdy. Pins are an especially great option for rentals and temporary fixes!

3. Overlap the paper slightly as needed.

4. Wrap them around a corner for added dimension.

Often the best personal touches
to a home have a story behind them!

Simplified
SPACES

Simplified
SPACES

Let's face it. Life can be hectic at times. Our days are busy and schedules are complicated, but designing our home or living in it shouldn't cause additional pressure. To combat the stress of the outside world and to make our home a refreshing escape, our design choices can reflect intentional order and simplicity.

Perfection can bring its own anxieties, so instead of endeavoring to create a perfect home, focus on the basics of what really matters to you. Create a backdrop where you can relax, feel at peace, and just be yourself.

There are many simple techniques you can use to streamline your style and pull together what you love. A home doesn't have to be complicated to be beautiful. Just as finding a place for everything and putting everything in its place will bring order to a cluttered room; simplifying your color scheme, your furniture, or your accessories can bring cohesion to your style and less stress to the process.

Focus on simple steps and improvements that will make a significant impact on how you live. The way you set up your home can make you feel either disorganized or inspired. A simplified space and ongoing, intentional style decisions will make the most of what you have and create a haven you'll enjoy.

Let's explore ways to simplify and beautify our home!

22 | DESIGNATE A PURPOSE FOR A ROOM

Approach the decor of a room with intention. Evaluate its purpose and then how to serve that purpose with its furniture and flow. If you get stuck, empty the space and start re-envisioning it with your needs in mind. Forget how the room was labeled in the floor plans. What do *you* want and need this room to be? For example, if your family never uses your dining room, and you're in desperate need of a homeschooling space or a home office, then look at that dining area with new eyes. Once you know the purpose of a room, a new plan will evolve, and a better use of your home will too.

What kind of space will add joy to your life and more life to your home? To get your creative juices flowing, here are some possible rooms you might be in need of:

study room	craft or sewing area
library	sitting room
dining nook	media room
home office	game room
family room	workout space
play area	storage area
writing room	walk-in closet

23 | INSPIRE YOUR ROOMS, INSPIRE YOUR LIFE

Inspired rooms don't have to be complicated or expensive to pull together. Keep it simple! If you want to live authentically, give yourself permission to eliminate the stress of furnishing your home according to style trends or your own expectations. Enjoy simplicity and see how your home will inspire you. Wander through these three easy room refreshes. Do something simple this week to renew one of your rooms.

BEDROOM

Use unexpected furniture. Maybe mix up nightstands by using a dresser for one and a small bookshelf as the other. This will help create a collected feel when combined with a traditional piece.

Layer a fluffy duvet and a mix of pillows. Atop of a cozy duvet, a variety of throw pillows will add dimension and a touch of pure luxury.

Sprinkle the personal throughout. It's your bedroom, so make it personal! Bring in accessories, books, and framed art and photos that speak to your heart and life's journey.

LIVING ROOM

Revive saggy cushions. Add foam pieces or other stuffing to zippered cushions. If they are sewn, then release part of the seam, fill, then re-stitch. They will look and feel much better.

Brighten your throw pillows. Buy or make new pillow coverings that add a color or pattern to your living or family room. For little or no money, you have a big payoff in personality.

Add flair to your floor. A new rug or one swapped out from another room will instantly connect the room elements in a new way. Shift toward a different depth of color tone or from a flat rug to one highly textured for even more of a change.

KITCHEN

Keep the sink clear. This one habit will make your space feel lighter and smell better, and it will welcome you back with cheer for the next mealtime.

Display your cookbook collection. Add colorful bookends—or kitchenware items as your bookends. This visual gathering will inspire a shelf or nook...and you!

Note to self: Create a garden. Bring warmth to your functional spaces. A memo board with uplifting notes and a kitchen garden of herbs are signs of a nurtured life.

24 | THINK IN THREES

See how the rule of three can give you the starting place you've been looking for.

FURNITURE

+ Have the pieces fill no more than two-thirds of your room.

+ Choose a coffee table that is approximately two-thirds as wide as your sofa.

+ A zone that has three pieces of furniture will be visually appealing.

WALL ACCESSORIES

+ Hang artwork or mirrors that are about two-thirds the width of whatever is below them.

+ Create an attractive gallery wall by envisioning a grid on the wall of three rows of three equally sized squares. The center square is your focal point. Hang various sizes of art at each of the intersecting corners.

COLOR

+ An easy interior design equation for your color palette is 60-30-10. The main room color should cover about 60 percent of the room, the secondary color should make up 30 percent, and the accent color is the remaining 10 percent.

+ Using a color three times in fabrics, backdrop elements, or accessory displays creates a cohesive feel in a room.

TEXTURE

+ Every room should have at least three varying textures to bring interest to the space.

+ If your tablescape or shelf surface is lacking substance, cluster objects made of three different textures for display. Consider glass, shells, and a candle. Or wood, stone, and a shiny metal.

25 | UNITE A ROOM WITH REPETITION

Repeated elements unite even the most eclectic rooms.

+ A pair of matching lamps or pillows offer symmetry.

+ Repetition of similar frames on the wall present a soothing backdrop.

+ Numerous white areas will tie together a room full of varied color and pattern.

+ Furniture pieces with a shared fabric pattern or color combination feel intentional.

+ Multiple accessories of a common material, such as glass, lead the eyes around a room.

+ Repeated visual weight provides balance. If you have a large window on one side of the room, counter it with a piece of furniture of similar visual significance on the other side.

26 | INVENT MINI DESTINATIONS

Shaping destinations in your home is a simple way to begin the process of creating the home you dream of. Break each room into several mini areas by defining a purpose for each. Special destinations within the home offer a sense of peace and invitation for you and guests. What kind of destination could transform an underused or cluttered space into a peaceful, purposeful corner?

MINI DESTINATIONS

coffee station	homework zone
reading corner	music area
sewing nook	command center

Mini destinations work well throughout your home, including the kitchen, garage, and outdoor spaces. Once you identify the purpose for your destination, you can create it in a day or an afternoon as you:

+ Clear clutter.

+ Evaluate any problems, such as a lack of light or lack of storage.

+ Introduce solutions that add beauty, not clutter.

+ Choose furniture pieces that suit the size of the space.

+ Assign only one corner or room as a particular kind of station, at least initially.

27 | REARRANGE FOR A WHOLE NEW LOOK

Are you bored with your space? Rather than shopping for all new furniture to change your look, recharge your energy and vision for your home by hunting for treasures around your house to rearrange what you have. The secret to successfully reimagining a space is to be willing to *set aside what is expected* or what you are *used to using* in other rooms of the house in order to try something new.

How could a corner of your home be used more effectively? What would inspire you to enjoy this space more in this season? Try a new furniture arrangement, a fresh color combination, different accessories, or an entirely new purpose for a space!

28 | SHAKE IT UP WITH UNEXPECTED FURNITURE

Chances are that most people have a sofa, coffee table, and chair in their living room. But why not think outside the box to find unique functional pieces that can add more charm and personality?

Here are some pieces you might have or can find in secondhand stores. How could any of these pieces be brought in to your room and repurposed or restyled to be used a functional way? Mix and match to create something new or assign an old piece a new function:

vintage sewing table	dresser
garden stool	window frame
antique secretary desk	potting table
picnic basket	steamer trunk
bar cart	leather suitcase or briefcase
hutch from a china cabinet	school desk
round metal tray	vintage ladder
buffet cabinet	wood chair
milk crate	large wood cable spool
vintage door	woven baskets

Don't forget a signature piece! Enhance a room by adding a signature piece of furniture. This is an item that—because of its color, shape, style, size, element of surprise, or striking presence—offers a wow factor. Multiple signature pieces in a room will make you and guests dizzy, but one well-chosen piece will draw the eye, spark conversation, and infuse your space with energy.

29 | EVERYTHING NEEDS A HOME

The secret to an orderly home is to ruthlessly declutter what you don't use or love and efficiently contain the things you do. Solutions can involve detailed storage systems, but sometimes they are the most simple of solutions, such as a tray, a basket, or a small box. How you organize isn't as important as the visual impact and function of what you have. Your home will be more beautiful when everything has a home and everything is in its place! Find systems and containers that reflect your personality, suit your style, and make your home more efficient.

EVERYDAY ITEM	SIMPLE STORAGE SOLUTION
Earrings, bracelets, and rings	Dipping bowls or small compartments in a drawer
Extra throw blankets	Leaning, decorative ladder or basket
Cleaning supplies	Over-the-door shoe organizer
Paper keepsakes	Labeled binders or lidded box
Vitamins and medications	Lazy Susan in a cupboard
Wayward office supplies	Shallow drawers or tiered organizer
Reusable grocery bags	Designated hooks in the pantry or entry
Kitchen dish towel	Self-adhesive hook on the side of a cabinet
Gift wrap supplies	Under-the-bed boxes
Bathroom toiletries	Rolling cart

Your home will be more beautiful when everything has a home and everything is in its place!

Creative
CONCEALMENTS

Creative
CONCEALMENTS

So, your room isn't perfect? Your windows are too small or your fire-place is off center. Maybe your room is awkwardly shaped, or you have too many doorways. Maybe your ceilings are low or too high. Who was the brilliant one who put the air conditioner in the middle of the wall or tiled that niche with the ugliest selection imaginable? And for the love of all things, why are there no closets in this house?

Welcome to the club. Most of us have imperfect spaces.

Most of us live in a home designed by or for someone else, so we need the freedom to redesign it to suit our needs. We won't feel more comfortable in our home by avoiding the glaring things we don't like or trying to fit our worldly belongings into someone else's limited version of space. We can make this house our home and love living in it!

Easier said than done, right?

Fortunately, home improvement doesn't always require a remodel. There are plenty of ways to creatively conceal awkward features and enhance the visual impact and function of each room. A good starting goal is to challenge yourself to make things *better than they were*. That takes the pressure off, doesn't it? But don't limit your creative potential. You have the power to take that room from "What were they thinking?" to "I can't even believe this is the same room!"

30 | DIRECT THE EYE WITH FOCAL POINTS

Does your room have a visually impactful focal point? In a good way? The focal point of a room should never be something unattractive. If you can't look away from that weirdly sized window or the world's most hideous built-in, then your job is to creatively update or disguise the feature you don't like or create a new focal point that says, "LOOK HERE!" to direct eyes toward a feature you do love.

Our living room had a fireplace we didn't love. The placement was off balance, and the stone and grout had a distracting pink hue. Every time we entered the space, it conflicted with the look we wanted. It incorrectly defined our style.

Without a remodel, we were able to minimize the design woes of the fireplace. We painted the stones a soft white to better blend in with the color on the plaster walls. Then we simply rearranged the furniture to balance the fireplace and created a conversation area around it. How can you redirect the line of sight in a room away from a less than lovely focal point?

AFTER

BEFORE

31 | HIDE DISTRACTIONS WITH EVERYDAY CONCEALERS

What feature of your home seems worn or awkward and in need of a creative concealment?

CHALLENGE	EVERYDAY CONCEALER
Chaotic, open storage area?	Hang a curtain.
Tired kitchen cupboards?	Paint the fronts or add new doors to the original cabinet boxes.
Ugly cords?	Hide them behind plants and baskets.
Wimpy, worn baseboards?	Paint them to match the walls.
Sloping floor?	Put taller pieces of furniture on the low side for visual balance.

More solutions to get your ideas flowing!

+ Rugs layered or rearranged can hide stained or worn wood or carpeted floors.

+ Fabric panels or hung rectangular tablecloths can enclose basement laundry areas or create makeshift closets.

+ Framed paintings, clocks, or rustic baskets can hide wall imperfections.

+ A simple coat of paint or stain refreshes unsightly furniture.

+ Potted vines, lattice panels, or trellises create private outdoor spaces and block unsightly views.

+ Paint unites mismatched pieces—or different colors can make similar pieces eclectic.

+ Charming shutters, blinds, or stained glass can conceal less than lovely views.

+ Faux board-and-batten or tin ceiling tiles add non-permanent architectural detail.

+ Old doors or a curtain hung behind a bed can give the illusion of a headboard.

+ Glaze or paint applied in varied brushstrokes creates a patina and hides uneven plaster or other wall flaws. Layer a couple colors for more distraction.

+ Outdoor light fixtures used indoors are strong focal points to detract from in-process areas.

+ Chalkboard paint can give fun life and versatility to flawed or ugly doors.

32 | SELECT DECOR-FRIENDLY STORAGE SOLUTIONS

We all have "stuff" in our home that we need, but let's be honest. All of that stuff usually detracts from the style and mood we are trying to create. We don't need to resign ourselves to a clutter-filled room, closet, or drawer that has become part of life. Discover ways to hide and store some of your most-used items while adding style to your home.

+ Hooks can hold aprons or mugs in the kitchen.

+ A wall-mounted shelf can display your prettiest bowls.

+ An old dresser can be spruced up to hold gloves and scarves in the entry.

+ Lidded baskets can hold surplus kitchen supplies.

+ A secretary desk could hold dishes, silverware, and placemats.

+ Clear storage drawers can categorize makeup or beauty products.

+ Fabric or metal magazine holders can be used to organize items in a closet.

+ A window box could be hung to hold towels and bathroom necessities.

+ A round-lidded ottoman can store your craft supplies.

+ Desktop mail organizers can hold bills.

+ Muffin tins could hold small accessories in a drawer.

+ A medicine cabinet can be hung for concealed bathroom storage.

+ Glass canisters can be kept on the counter for flour and sugar.

+ A pretty pottery crock can hold extra wooden spoons.

+ Kids' toys can be kept in fabric bins or woven baskets.

+ An old wooden ladder could be hung on the ceiling to hold pots and pans in the kitchen or set against a wall for favorite quilts.

+ Shallow wood boxes can be hung on the wall for glass jars of spices in the kitchen or cosmetics in the bathroom.

+ A coffee table trunk could hide electronics in a family room or keep blankets in a bedroom.

+ Dog food could be kept in lidded metal buckets.

+ Cute flowerpots or jars can hold pens and highlighters on a desk.

+ Favorite teacups or small bowls can hold paperclips or other necessities in drawers.

+ A small cabinet in the dining room could hold glassware.

+ A pretty lidded box could conceal necessities on an open nightstand.

+ A decorative tray can corral jewelry.

+ Fabric-covered containers can hold office supplies, notecards, or mementos.

+ A basket can hold reading material by the bed or a favorite chair.

+ An antique armoire could be repurposed as a clothes closet.

33 | DESIGN "COZY" INTO LARGE ROOMS

Big rooms are wonderful for entertaining, but they aren't always cozy or functional for day-to-day living. Simple ideas will help you and your family fully use and enjoy a large space.

Designate zones. Distinct zones bring intention to a large space. Consider a media or game zone, conversation area, dining area, or a reading nook. Be sure to include a lighting source for a zone.

Divide the space visually. Pillars, ceiling beams, or half walls are permanent division options. Fluid choices include area rugs, a chaise lounge or sofa, wallpaper transitions, large plants, or screens. Paint the ceiling a shade or two darker to divide and cozy up a room.

Anchor areas. Several significant pieces, such as a sectional, large coffee table, built-in bookcase, or a piano, will anchor a room and allow places for smaller pieces to be nestled in and not lost.

Increase the scale. Opt for proportionate, taller furniture, especially if you have vaulted ceilings. Consider a large bookcase, an armoire, and chairs and sofas with tall backs.

Double up. Center a conversation area with two matching square ottomans in the center. Use two area rugs to shape two different zones. Double up with a pair of chairs, two matching large lamps, etc.

Avoid wall hugging. Bring furniture in around a focal point, such as a fireplace. Save wall space for art, buffets, consoles, shelving, or additional conversation areas.

Go bigger. Up your game and choose bigger, bolder art and accessories. Go with extra big frames and/or add larger matting to showcase art and photos. Consider a vibrant, large-image painting.

Connect with texture. If your room feels cold or cavernous, bring in additional layers of curtain panels, throw blankets, rugs, and upholstered pieces. Repeated patterns or colors will unite the space.

34 | STREAMLINE SMALL SPACES

Make room for what you love. Pare down or consolidate items. What could you get rid of? What can you store out of sight to eliminate clutter? Limit your number of storage options too.

Look up. Draw the line of sight upward with tall mirrors and furniture, a wall gallery, painted vertical stripes, striped curtains, or drapes hung above the window frame.

Be intentional. Conceal clutter in small spaces. Establish order in an entry area with a memo board, a dresser, and a key rack. Create an office nook with a work station on casters or a laptop in a secretary hutch. Add hooks for storage and wall shelves for visual displays.

Build it in. Consider a built-in bookcase or storage window seat to ease visual clutter. Free-standing units nestled into a corner or against a wall offer similar benefits.

Get grounded. In an awkwardly shaped room, a horizontal-striped rug can help visually center and widen your space. A statement light fixture can bring clarity and style to an uninspired room.

Choose functional furniture. The right pieces can make all the difference:

+ tall and narrow shelving

+ round ottomans or coffee tables

+ nesting tables

+ small scale and armless pieces

+ drop-leaf dining tables, desk stations, or side tables

+ corner storage pieces

+ storage containers that fit under beds or couches

+ mirrors to expand visual space

+ dual-function selections (a dining room cabinet that offers space for dish storage and a surface for serving)

Bring in the benches. Benches are one of the most versatile pieces for any home. Use them for storage, seating, shelving, tables, foot stools, and zone dividers.

35 | EMBELLISH YOUR FURNITURE

Don't buy something new when you can refresh what you have. Give what you have some love. Enjoy the process and result of trying something different!

+ Dab metallic paint on handles or other hardware for a new look.

+ Paper the interior of an open bookcase with gift wrap, maps, wall paper, or ornate scrapbook paper.

+ Drape fabric over a lackluster chair as a slipcover. Look at drapes, sheets, and bolts of fabric as potential material for this furniture refresh! (A soft drop cloth can even be fashioned as a slipcover to conceal a dated upholstered ottoman.)

Give what you have some love.

Touchable
TEXTURES

Touchable TEXTURES

Your favorite destinations are filled with an interesting mix of textures. Texture is everywhere in nature! Imagine the tactile experience of a walk on the beach. You feel the warm grains of sand beneath your feet and the contrast of the cool glassy tide pools. You notice the texture of the foam that bubbles on the waves and the white fluffy clouds floating effortlessly across the clear blue sky. The mix of jagged rocks and smooth driftwood are a significant part of the experience.

Just as the combination of organic elements is foundational to our sense of enjoyment and pleasure in nature, they are essential to our delight in our home. If you sense something is missing in your own space, you might only need to create more complex layers of tactile and visual texture.

To establish an inviting experience, each room in your home should include a variety of touchable materials, accessories, and points of interest. Incorporating a carefully chosen mix of textures will delight your eyes as well as bring comfort to the space.

Each piece plays a significant part in the overall look and feel of your home. The hardware you love, the fabrics you select, the furniture and useful items within help create an experience. How you arrange the elements and combine the functional and decorative pieces in your space builds layers of texture and contrast.

While it might seem complicated to create a space with many layers, you don't have to be a professional to pull together a well-designed room. There are many easy ways and simple guidelines to add depth to your style and touchable texture to your home.

36 INTRODUCE TEXTURE WITH INTENTION

Add texture with intention by incorporating a variety of materials into your floor and wall treatments, furniture, lighting, decorative accessories, and fabrics. The options are endless!

wood	stone	linen	corduroy	canvas
rattan	mirror	leather	cable knit	crewel
paint	metal	suede	flannel	lace
acrylic	ceramic	silk	fleece	jute
lacquer	crystal	velvet	wool	beads
glass	pottery	faux fur	chenille	cork
marble	tweed	cashmere	chambray	concrete

37 | TRANSFORM A SPACE WITH PILLOWS AND THROWS

Changing and adding pillows is one of the most versatile ways to refresh a room. Not only do they provide comfort and a finishing touch, they can add pizazz to an otherwise blah space or tone down a busy room. The right mix of shapes, sizes, colors, and patterns can bring your look together with your unique flair.

+ Select pillows that are appropriately sized and shaped both visually and functionally for your space. Accent pillows should not be too small. A 20" pillow works for most sofas.

+ Oblong or round pillows are great accent pillows at the center of a sofa, bed or on chairs.

+ For an extra plush look, invest in down or down-blend pillows. Down lasts far longer than foam inserts and has a softer look.

+ To stretch your seasonal design options, use removable pillow covers. For the fullest look, use a down-blend insert one size bigger than your cover.

+ Vary the scale of your pillow patterns so the overall effect in the room is pleasing.

+ Solid pillows can tone down a room full of pattern as well as help define a cohesive palette.

+ Select a unified color scheme for all of the pillows in a room.

+ If you mix pillow patterns, select one hue that will be your common denominator.

+ Select prints with tone-on-tone or neutral colors for a less busy look.

+ Odd numbers of pillows and symmetrical placement on a sofa are visually pleasing.

+ If you use only two pillows on a sofa, choose one solid and one patterned for visual interest.

+ Add in pillows with texture too! Think about fur, knit, and silky options for a fun mix.

+ Arrange your pillows with a 2-2-1 formula. Two matching, equally sized and shaped pillows on either end of a sofa; two smaller, like-sized pillows in a different fabric next to them; and one smaller accent pillow in the middle. Try one of these coordinating combinations:

Outer pillows: matching, polka-dot patterned 22"-26" square pillows

Next: matching, floral 20" square pillows

Middle: one solid 12" x 20"

Outer pillows: matching, solid 20" square pillows

Next: matching, striped, or plaid 20" square pillows in coordinating colors

Middle: one large-scale floral 12" x 20" pillow

+ Try a 2-1 combination for smaller couches or love seats.

38 | BALANCE WITH CONTRAST

What stands out as your dominant textures and tones? Add in whatever contrasting textures will provide balance. Surprisingly, contrast can be the key to a welcoming harmony in a room.

+ Complement a room of primarily painted furniture pieces with those that are natural wood or glass and vice versa.

+ Enhance a room that has a lot of fabric and softness with a basket, large shell, collection of stones, or a natural fiber rug.

+ Get creative with different pairings to see what you enjoy.

+ Brighten a dark room with light-colored furniture or accessories.

+ Place lamps where they will provide ambient light to soften starkness or shadows and clear the black holes.

+ Balance neutrals with color and off-set a colorful room with neutrals.

+ Contrast the smooth sheen of silverware and ceramic plates with table runners, place mats, and napkins in natural and textured materials.

+ Bring in plants, such as a potted fern, bouquet of flowers, or a gathering of potted succulents, to provide texture and life to a furnished space.

CREATIVE CONTRASTS

solid, sleek items with pieces that have a patina

sheens with matted finishes and fibrous textures

woven blankets with soft fleece or silky choices

natural elements with decor bling (chandeliers, shiny metal accessories and hardware, colored glass, or metal furniture trim)

39 | PLAY WITH PATTERNS

A mix of patterns can make a room feel vibrant and welcoming. Here are some secrets for successful pattern mixing!

Decide the mood. If you want a lively space, a mix of colors and patterns bring energy to a room. If you crave calm, choose subtle patterns or tone-on-tone, textured elements.

Anchor with neutrals. A solid rug, neutral-fabric ottoman, or a simplified paint palette will balance lively elements. If you have patterned furniture, use neutrals to create a new foundation for those existing patterns.

Plan your pattern palette. Select a couple of colors (for instance, shades of blue and white or a mix of green, blue, and white) and stick to that limited color scheme as you add patterned items. Pare away existing patterns that don't work with the new plan.

Start with a formula. Mix patterns with confidence by using a simple guideline:

> a solid + a small scale + a large scale

For example, if you choose shades of blue, gray, and white, start with a solid light blue pillow. Next, add a small-scale pattern in navy blue and white (such as a tiny polka-dot print). Then add a large-scale light blue, white, and dark gray pillow (perhaps a floral).

Experiment for fun. Once you've mastered the basics, mix in additional colors and several scales of patterns.

Visualize the whole picture. Evaluate all the patterns in a room as a whole. Do they work together? Note elements that will read as a pattern, such as flooring materials (textured or patterned wood, rugs, or tile), furnishings (notice lines or intricate shapes), light fixtures, wall coverings, cabinets, counters, and ceilings.

Take pictures of your patterns. Refer to these photos when considering a purchase to complement your look. Or photograph items at the store to evaluate at home.

40 | LEAN OBJECTS FOR EASE AND BEAUTY

Leaning a few objects against walls or other backdrops creates visual texture. I started to lean items when a previous home had plaster too fragile to support hanging items. I loved the effect so much that, to this day, it's one of my favorite decor tips.

WHY?

+ easy to change up

+ hides unsightly items, such as outlets, vents, and plaster or flooring flaws

+ more dimension, variance, interest, and casual charm

+ more angle options than hanging allows

WHAT?

+ framed artwork or photos

+ canvassed pieces, such as lettered art

+ architectural pieces, such as shutters

+ mirrors

+ metal or wood signs

+ stained glass panels

+ antique washboards

+ intricate iron wall art

+ vintage doors, window frames, ladders

+ chalkboard panels

+ smaller accessories, photos, or paintings next to larger pieces

WHERE?

+ back of bookshelves

+ tabletops

+ mantels

+ windowsills

+ floors

+ stair landings

HOW?

+ Bigger, heavier architectural pieces or mirrors can lean by themselves without additional layers, while smaller artwork usually looks best with multiple pieces layered and overlapped.

+ Place shorter accessories or stacked books in front of a taller leaning or background piece.

+ Stabilize smaller pieces with sticky tack to keep them from slipping and sliding.

+ Secure larger elements for safety with a picture hook or Command Strips (Velcro hangers).

+ When leaning mirrors, always check to see what you are reflecting in them.

41 | LAYER YOUR LINENS

Pamper yourself with the warmth and texture of layered bedding. A mix of fabrics creates a visually luxurious style and a refreshing sleep experience each night. Here are three layers for a cozy and textured bed.

1. **Comfortable Sheets.** When you can, invest in comfortable, high-quality, higher-thread-count sheets. You can choose simple white or a solid color and add pattern and texture with other bedding or try the reverse. Use solids and textures on the top layers and have the patterns surprise you when you pull back the covers! Try sheets in fun stripes, florals, or polka dots.

2. **Mix of Blankets.** For visual interest and comfort flexibility, layer a blanket and then a lightweight quilt over the sheets. For extra coziness, add an additional fluffy duvet or throw blanket loosely folded or draped at the end of the bed.

3. **Plenty of Pillows.** Layers of pillows will add height and dimension to your bed. For a stylishly layered queen bed, select a combination of at least two Euro-style pillows (big square pillows), two standard pillows with shams, and a center accent pillow. For a playful look, mix patterned or colored shams. Create the feel you love with different pillow fabric textures: grain sack, faux fur, knit covers, or pillows with a surprising metallic sheen.

42 | WARM UP WITH WOOD

A single element can transform a space. Wood will add texture, beauty, and visual interest. Here are some ways to warm up your room.

ACCESSORIES

Enhance your kitchen with wood cutting boards, wood spoons, and wood bowls. Add subtle touches to other rooms with crates and woven baskets, and frames and wood sculptures.

FLOORS, WALLS, AND WINDOW

Warmth and texture added to your beautiful backdrops, from floor to ceiling, will make your home cozy: bamboo, woven rugs; wood paneling and molding; blinds, curtain rods, and finials. We used a tree branch as a curtain rod in my son's former room for a rustic touch.

FURNITURE

Any room can be warmed up with one piece of wood furniture. Consider a table or chair for a gathering area, an island for your kitchen, a headboard for the bedroom, and a wood storage element in your bathroom.

How do you want to warm up your style?

Artful
ACCESSORIES

Artful
ACCESSORIES

People who collect treasures as they experience life adventures can create such personal and welcoming homes! The most interesting rooms will tell the most fascinating tales. Your story is uniquely yours to tell, whether you have traveled the world or made a home in one place. The practical elements you use every day and the accessories you gather over time should reflect your personal history, taste, and passions.

Your style should be ever evolving as you grow and your taste is refined. Don't rush the process! Your home should not be a static snapshot of the person you were at one point in time. Enjoy the adventure of continually refreshing your space as you collect, display, and arrange accessories and functional elements that speak to you so they can breathe new life and soul into your home.

43 | MAKE A STATEMENT

Knickknacks might catch our eye when we are shopping, but little odds and ends can feel lost in a larger room. Too many pieces spread out on every surface will make a room feel more cluttered than decorated. To unify your space, start with a clean slate. Remove the accessories from each surface. Replace accessories by adopting the "less is more" principle. How could you make bolder design statements with fewer pieces? Train your eye to carefully edit what you display in a room and then make a statement with a standout piece or two:

+ a large ceramic container on an entry table

+ a large pair of candlesticks on a mantel

+ an oversized light in your dining area

+ a substantial potted plant in a corner

+ a large mirror in your living room

+ a large scale art canvas

Smaller pieces can still find a home. Arrange similar items together on a tray or area of a surface for more visibility. Groupings of frames, figurines, books, or dishes can be presented as a collection for a bigger impact.

44 | BEAUTIFY REAL LIFE

Those everyday items you and your family reach for throughout the day can be your most important, most artful accessories. When you choose functional pieces that are beautiful, your home will be well decorated and tell your story even without decorative tchotchkes. Select practical items in styles, colors, and patterns that inspire you. Coordinate collections of everyday necessities and display them creatively so they will contribute to your overall look. Keep your decorative elements simple and focus on making real life beautiful.

EVERYDAY ON DISPLAY

dishes	hooks
pitchers	candlesticks and holders
colorful mugs and teacups	tote bags
kitchenware	umbrella stands
plates	mirrors
serving trays	jewelry boxes
chalkboards	wooden game boards
books and bookends	heirlooms or family hand-me-downs
baskets	quilts

45 | COLLECT 7 SIMPLE DECOR ACCESSORIES

The look and feel of your home will develop over time. Along the way, choose a few favorite accessories to collect. These 7 decor items are easy to find and simple to add to any room's look.

1. **Plates and Platters.** Collect pretty plates in your favorite colors and patterns for your table and your walls! To save space, use white plates and platters for everyday use and mix in specialty items.

2. **Metal Pieces.** Hang attractive pots and pans on racks or stack them for display on shelves.

3. **Throw Blankets.** Gather quilts or blankets of varying textures and colors to drape over a chair or fold and stack on a shelf as a decorative element.

4. Artwork. Collect art to commemorate significant events, such as anniversaries and special family moments. Look for prints, postcards, greetings cards, maps, or books.

5. Vases and Vessels. Whether you fill them with objects or leave them empty, special vases and vessels are statement accents for shelves, mantels, or entryway surfaces.

6. Baskets. Handmade woven baskets can be useful to carry or corral wayward pieces or to create a home for less attractive items. Even hang them on your wall as unexpected art!

7. Books. Vintage or collectible books add personality and texture to tabletops or shelving to elevate other special items on surfaces, making a house feel like a lived-in home.

46 | GO ON A TREASURE HUNT

Swap accessories between rooms for immediate, no-cost makeovers. When you are ready to refresh a space, take a look through your cabinets, closets, other rooms, and yard for cool stuff to use in a new way. Just because an item has sat in the same spot for years doesn't mean it has to stay put. You'll never know what will work until you try it! You might be surprised how much more you'll love your space if you simply move accessories around. Try these unexpected pieces in a new location:

a twisty branch	an old gate or window frame
table runners	a collection of postcards
a wood or glass box	musical instruments
pretty scarves	lamps or lampshades

47 | DIY: CREATE SENTIMENTAL ART

We all have little treasures that spark special memories, but how often do those items see the light of day? Usually they are stuffed in boxes, out of sight. Make your memories a part of your life. Create sentimental art to use as a statement piece or as a focal point for a gallery wall.

For this DIY, select items that are from meaningful people or moments: the blouse you wore when your husband proposed, your daughter's newborn hat, your grandma's doilies, an uncle's plaid shirt, your mom's wedding gloves, or a favorite piece of jewelry that you don't wear anymore.

1. Gather the meaningful pieces you want to display as art.

2. Find a linen place mat or piece of wrapping paper to be the backdrop.

3. Affix the backdrop to the back of the frame or to a piece of sturdy foam board with fabric glue.

4. Tack the memento to the backing, use fabric glue, decorative pushpins, or inconspicuous staples.

5. Frame the art, or use bull clips or even clipboards to showcase your art! Leave off the glass if your art is dimensional.

6. Hang this new art in a geometric grid or a free flowing gallery wall or just highlight one or two special pieces together.

48 | DISPLAY WITH DIMENSION

A few simple tips will help you add style and character to your displays.

Design high to low and front to back. A display will usually look best when you use accessories in different heights, decorating high to low or layering against a wall or shelf front to back. Tall items can be vases, a leaning frame, a willow branch in a glass jug, or a cluster of smaller items on top of a stack of books or plates. Then mix in the lower accessories for a visually interesting effect.

Vary the impact. Add round items to soften straight lines, include various thicknesses and sizes, pair opposite textures, include an organic element, and mix in the unexpected.

Create a focal point. A mirror or piece of framed artwork hung above a mantel or a shelving unit automatically creates an interesting focal point *and* a backdrop for the accessories you place on that surface.

49 DECORATE WITH NATURAL ELEMENTS

Including nature in your home's decor is one of the easiest, least expensive, and most attractive ways to blend any season with your style.

FLOWERS IN UNIQUE CONTAINERS

Place your blooms in a coffee tin, galvanized bucket, soup tureen, pitcher, antique toolbox, or a decorative bowl.

DRIFTWOOD, BRANCHES, OR ANTLERS

Try leaning a tall branch in a corner. Use a piece of driftwood as a simple centerpiece or even as an organic curtain rod. Add antlers to a gallery wall for a three dimensional, natural element.

MIXED ELEMENTS

Fill glass lamps or vases with pinecones, cinnamon sticks, shells, sand, moss, and ornaments during the holidays.

NATURAL TONES AND TEXTURES

Decorate with nature's colors and materials. Consider leather, rattan, and wood. Mixing and matching neutral shades and items will unite your look.

COASTAL INSPIRATIONS

If you love the beach the way I do, incorporate coastal elements in your decor. Use subtle colors of the sea, starfish, shell bowls, or artwork depicting ocean scenes.

SIMPLE GREENERY

Place a plant clipping from your yard in a glass jug or jar. Air plants are an easy option and virtually impossible to kill (a win-win). Plant succulents in a teacup collection for a pretty touch.

NATURAL CENTERPIECES

Fill a tray, bowl, or wreath with pebbles and candles. Border with fruit, moss, pinecones, etc. Cover a cake stand surface with these elements for a visual feast.

50 | FILL YOUR HOME WITH GRATITUDE

There are many ways to decorate your home. Each effort you make to improve your surroundings is a valuable one, but don't let unfinished projects or an unfulfilled wish list lessen the joy of having a place that embraces you, your family, and the guests who come and go. Make the time to enjoy and fully live in the spaces you create, filling your home with not only material possessions, but with a sense of gratitude for what you already have.

It's a haven.

It's a place for rest.

It's an expression of you.

It's an invitation to others.

It's a gift.

About the
AUTHOR

Melissa Michaels is the creator and author of the popular home decorating blog *The Inspired Room*, which inspires women to love the home they have. Since 2007 Melissa has been encouraging hundreds of thousands of readers a month with daily posts and inspiration for all things house and home. *The Inspired Room* was twice voted as the *Better Homes and Gardens* magazine Reader's Choice decorating blog.

Melissa lives with her husband, Jerry; their son, Luke; and two impossibly adorable Doodle pups, Jack and Lily, whose adventures are well loved and followed on their Facebook page (Facebook.com/jack.goldendoodle). The Michaels' daughters, Courtney and Kylee (and Kylee's husband, Lance), are an active part of *The Inspired Room*.

CONNECT WITH MELISSA AND OTHER HOME LOVERS

- The Inspired Room Blog - **theinspiredroom.net**
- **Subscribe** - Have new blog posts delivered to your inbox.
- **melissa@theinspiredroom.com**
- Facebook.com/**theinspiredroom**
- Instagram - **@theinspiredroom**
- Pinterest - **@theinspiredroom**

SIMPLY HOME

ORGANIZING

Melissa Michaels

TEN PEAKS PRESS®
EUGENE, OR

Published in association with William K. Jensen Literary Agency,
119 Bampton Court, Eugene, Oregon 97404

Cover and interior design by Faceout Studio
Kids' room photos by Cassie Kulp

For bulk or special sales, please call 1-800-547-8979.
Email: Customerservice@hhpbooks.com

TEN PEAKS PRESS is a federally registered trademark of The Hawkins Children's LLC.
Harvest House Publishers, Inc., is the exclusive licensee of this trademark.

SIMPLY HOME
Copyright © 2017, 2018 by Melissa Michaels
Published by Ten Peaks Press, an imprint of Harvest House Publishers
Eugene, Oregon 97408

ISBN 978-0-7369-8767-7 (hardcover)
Library of Congress Control Number: 2022952321

Previously published as *Simple Decorating* and *Simple Organizing* by Melissa Michaels

Printed in China

23 24 25 26 27 28 29 30 31 / RDS / 10 9 8 7 6 5 4 3 2 1

Contents

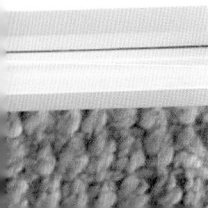

BATHROOMS 77

KIDS' ROOMS 93

HOME OFFICE & CREATIVE SPACES 107

CONCLUSION 123

MAKE THE MOST OF YOUR SPACE

Your home is your special place to live life. Whether you're living in your dream home or a small apartment, the same rule should apply to getting yourself organized: Make the most of the space you have.

Organization isn't just about setting up a storage system. It's about designing a home that truly reflects your family. By using pieces that are pleasing to your eye, you'll actually *enjoy* maintaining your space. The systems you select become a way to showcase your style and keep your home under control at the same time.

Best of all, as you organize your home, you also organize your life. You don't waste time searching for missing items. Your surfaces are clearer, so your mind feels clearer too. You're not afraid to entertain friends or neighbors. Your home won't be perfect, but that's okay. That's not the point. It will be presentable and comfortable and a place you're proud to call your own.

Tip: You can motivate yourself to further cleaning and decluttering by taking before-and-after photographs of your newly cleaned and organized area. Even if it isn't perfect, progress inspires!

As we journey through the spaces of our homes, beginning with the entryway, you'll begin to catch a vision of the best organizing plan for you and your loved ones. You may feel most at home with lots of empty space and room to breathe. Or you may be content with a cozy amount of treasures, wanting to be surrounded by a comfortable amount of stuff. No matter your preference, you'll learn to look at your home with a practiced eye, determining what you truly use and what you could do without.

After you've cleared the clutter, you can establish some simple habits and routines that keep your home—and your life—well ordered and organized. Simple organizing is about making the most of the space you have and creating a home that works for your family so you can get on to the most important things in life! The things that aren't *things* at all. That's the heart behind simple organizing.

Entrances

SET THE STAGE FOR A
WELCOMING HOME

When you visit homes you love, what do you feel as soon as you step into the entryway? What says welcome? What do you want your guests—as well as those who live in your home—to feel when they step into your entryway?

The entryway sets the tone for the rest of your home. You can ascertain a feeling of calm or chaos right from the start. A tiny entryway can look larger with the right organizing plan, and even a large entryway can appear cluttered when there's too much stuff in the mix.

Entrances also dictate the tone of our coming and going. If coats and backpacks and keys are easy to access, we can head out the door with a positive attitude. But if we're scrambling to find important papers and searching for a matching shoe, we're not going to start off our day on the right foot. Maybe even literally!

With simple storage solutions and a look at the big picture, the entryway can set the stage for a feeling of order in the rest of the home. No remodels or renovations are necessary to get organized. Use what you have—that's a theme throughout this book—and make the most of your space. That's the best way to create a warm welcome.

1 | START SMART

Take a look around your home. Do your spaces look tidy, organized, and welcoming? Or do clutter and chaos take center stage? Don't worry if you answered "clutter and chaos." You're not alone.

Every day we make choices that contribute to disorder in our homes. We put things down instead of putting them away. We fail to create designated spaces for our stuff. We put off picking up until the next day—and then we run out of time. And that's okay. We can't expect perfection every single day.

When you're not sure what to do first, set just one goal. When you're feeling wishy-washy or indecisive about what to do next, take one specific step. I recommend starting in your entryway—the space that visitors (and you and your family!) see when you first walk into your house. Then choose just one thing to improve or organize. It might be a pile of discarded shoes or a stack of mail or all the stuff you need to walk your dog.

You'll be successful in your organizing if you remember to let go of the perfect solution and commit to just a simple one. A foolproof way to do this is by setting goals that are SMART:

S—Specific: Get rid of the pile of shoes cluttering up the entry instead of simply lining them up over and over again.

M—Measurable: Pare down what is kept in this space, allowing only one pair of shoes per family member to be left in the entry.

A—Achievable: Find a storage system so you can keep the shoes in the entry but allow them to stay hidden.

R—Realistic: Don't set an unnecessary goal, such as designing an elaborate shoe storage system for multiple pairs of shoes per person. Fewer shoes and less mess in the entry is the goal, not more storage for more stuff.

T—Time Limited: Set a timeline for steps and completion, such as 30 minutes in the morning or afternoon.

Start with the entryway—and start SMART. Make a series of small, simple goals to kick out the chaos and get your home simply organized.

2 | FASHION A FABULOUS FRONT PORCH

First impressions. Curb appeal. Opening statement. If you're accustomed to entering your house through the garage or back door, you might not realize the impact your front porch makes on your entire home. Pop onto your porch and take a critical look. Is the Christmas wreath still up—and you're midway through February? Is the main focal point a massive mountain of kids' toys? Are empty pots or broken planters cluttering up valuable gathering space?

Prioritize organizing your front porch and giving your family and friends a little more room and reason to linger when the weather is nice. It's pretty incredible what eliminating excess clutter can do for adding a welcoming vibe. Even if your porch looks more like a small stoop, you can add curb appeal and function.

CLEAN SWEEP

The best way to bring order to your porch? Get everything off it—plants, furniture, kids' toys, mats, storage boxes. Sweep it clean (including around the frame of the front door), eliminate the cobwebs, scrub the house numbers, hose everything off, and get it looking like new. Then assess what you *truly* want to put back. Chances are you'll love how sparkling the empty space looks and won't be willing to return every item.

FEET FIRST

Either clean your front porch mat of all mud, dirt, and leaves, or splurge on a new one if the old one is beyond help. Fun patterns and styles can be found inexpensively at discount stores. You can even change them up to match the season.

TOY TAMER

While kids should be encouraged to play outdoors and provided with the necessary equipment, scattered toys can really ruin the look. Corral front yard toys in a big basket or bucket. Kids are capable of putting toys away if you provide simple instructions combined with an age-appropriate organizational system.

DOUBLE DUTY

Consider using simple benches or weatherproof outdoor furniture, such as an old table, vintage desk, crate, or unique shelving unit to add storage space for plants, decorative accents, or even creative shoe storage. Super functional and super cute!

SIMPLIFIED SEASONS

While decorating for the holidays is fun, it's easy to go overboard and not be able to keep up with it through the seasons. Give yourself permission to decorate your porch simply. Focus on natural decor you can enjoy for several months, such as potted plants or a simple wreath. A seasonal item or two can be gorgeous when displayed on your front porch and then composted or gotten rid of easily and without guilt when the season is over.

WELCOME YOURSELF LIKE A GUEST

3

When you walk through your front door multiple times each day, it's easy to not really see your house at all. You're thinking about the meal that needs to be prepared or the meeting you just had or the carpool you're scheduled to pick up.

Next time you come home, step into your entryway and look around. Ask yourself, *How would a guest feel if they were entering my home right now? Does the atmosphere feel chaotic or calm?* Treat your entry like a welcoming haven for yourself and for your family. Make it your favorite place to return to every day!

Realize that the impression you make in the entryway sets the impression for the rest of your house. What does your entry say about your home?

Focus on function. My family's home is happy, casual, and lively. Our small entry is designed to welcome people and pups alike. We keep our home streamlined but casual and informal. Organize your entryway to reflect your family, activities, and interests.

Simplify your stuff. Take five or ten minutes to note what doesn't belong. You can even grab a box or basket and start the decluttering process right then and there. Don't toss the box in the spare bedroom. Give unnecessary things away or recycle.

Think simple, attractive, and organized. A place for everything. What are your needs? Stylish baskets and aesthetically pleasing storage containers can transform a formerly disorderly space. Use what you have or shop in your own home for furniture and organizers to solve storage dilemmas.

Embrace the space you have. Even if you don't have a separate entryway, you can add hooks, a mirror, a rug, or a small bookcase near the door to create a feeling of a designated area. Shuffle things around until it seems just right.

4

ESTABLISH AN
ENTRY-LEVEL PLAN

Create a simple checklist you want to tackle so you can stay focused.

Choose a few daily tasks to keep the entry looking fresh and welcoming even during the craziest of weeks. Five fast minutes of sweeping, tidying, and dusting can actually make an amazing difference. If you can't tidy your entry in a matter of minutes, it's time to reevaluate your systems and come up with an easier plan.

Make it your mantra to put things away instead of putting them down. That takes a little more energy, but it will save you valuable minutes in the long run. Bonus: No time wasted tracking down missing items.

Look for the little things—keys, purses, pet leashes, phones, papers. These items tend to scatter and disappear. Designate easy-to-maintain spots for them. Look for trays, baskets, or hooks for your most-used items.

Plan a time during the week for returning everything to its proper place. Turn on some energetic music and get the entire family involved. Or even better, tidy as you go each day. Set up a plan and stick with it. Don't let clutter land and multiply.

Embrace the domino effect: Each positive organizing choice you make, no matter how small or seemingly inconsequential (such as hanging your keys on a hook every time you walk in the door), leads to new, positive choices and actions throughout the day. Make systems easy and practical so everyone in the family can learn to do the same.

Remember that it takes just one wrong decision to start things moving toward disorganization and clutter. A constantly growing pile of shoes, a stack of unopened mail, gloves and scarves tossed on a table...messes like these tend to spill out to other areas of your home.

Add seasonal style to your plan. It's fun to use seasonal decor in the entry-way—a vase of sunflowers in August, a few mini pumpkins in October, tulips in April. Using items from nature works well to reduce clutter because these decorations are temporary and don't need to be stored anywhere. Bonus: A pretty vase or vessel on an entry table can remind you to commit to keeping surfaces clear of clutter.

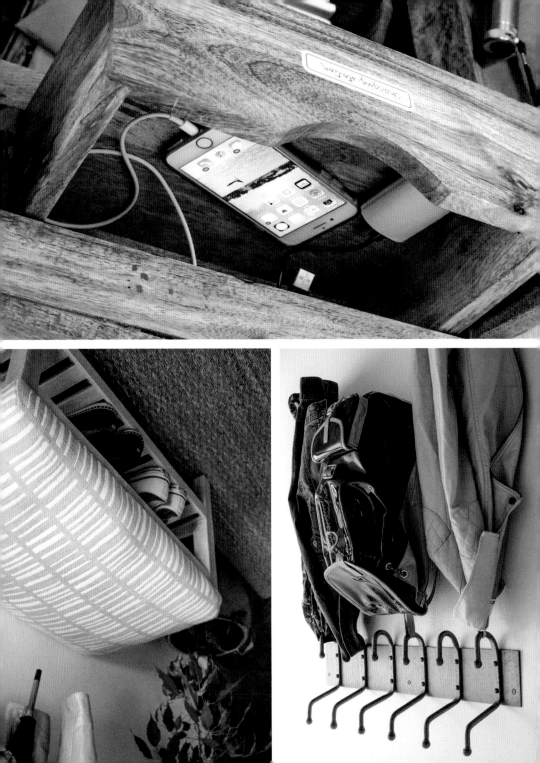

5

STRAIGHTEN UP A SMALL SPACE

No matter if your entryway is its own separate room or just the front of your living room, easy storage options help you make the most of this limited area. If you don't have a designated coat closet or enough room for everything you need to access, here are some practical ways to house necessities in a small space.

1. **Lidded boxes, baskets, and small trunks.** Search flea markets, garage sales, or your own closets for useful and pleasing storage options that hide piles of shoes, shopping bags, and winter essentials (such as scarves, hats, and gloves). A tall, open basket or metal container can make it easy to grab an umbrella on the way out the door.

2. **Small trays and bins.** Corral small wayward items—mail, school papers, items to return—in an attractive way. Small trays and bins can keep surfaces or shelves tidy.

3. **Expand your storage.** If your entryway doesn't have enough space for what you need, look for nearby options in adjoining spaces. A dresser in the living room, a guest room closet, or a linen cabinet in a hall can be repurposed as entryway storage space.

4. **Pet-gear crate.** If you're a dog owner like me, you know it's important to have access to going-for-a-walk gear, such as raincoats (yes, our dogs have raincoats for rainy days), harnesses, or flashlights for nighttime walks.

5. **The perfect piece.** Furniture can streamline storage for so many entryway necessities. Look for a shallow cabinet, a small dresser, a slim table with storage below, or a bench with storage or coat rack above.

6. **Creative hangers.** Create more space by getting things up and out of the way. Fashion an original coat hanger for your wall with just about anything (shutters, an old door, a weathered plank of wood) and a few functional, attractive hooks. Remember, hangers aren't just for coats. They're also great for bags, scarves, totes, purses, and anything else that needs a home up and out of the way.

6 | PREP YOUR PURSE

When you're busy coming and going, a fully prepped and organized purse is crucial to managing your time and your life well. Having a special hook for your purse in the entry area makes it super easy to grab and go (no more running late due to searching the house for a wayward pocketbook!).

Tidy up your purse and declutter your wallet to prepare yourself for whatever the day brings—whether that's a business meeting or a class or a volunteer activity. Remember, an organized purse puts you further along the path to an organized life!

1. Clear out your purse completely, including your wallet, emptying all pockets and containers.

2. Recycle wrappers and trash and file away all necessary receipts and papers.

3. Put essential cash, debit or credit cards, and health cards back into your wallet.

4. Add small, zippered pouches to corral loose items for better organization and easier access (makeup, reward cards, coins, and personal items).

5. Designate a particular pocket for your cell phone and keys so you can easily grab them when needed. Slip in a small notebook for jotting down essential notes or shopping needs.

6. Create your own little purse-sized emergency kit so you're prepared for anything. Include a few first aid supplies (such as Band-Aids and pain medication), toiletries, laundry pen, mints, and cash.

You can also use these steps when you're cleaning out tote bags, backpacks, or beach bags that tend to get cluttered and messy. A quick weekly upkeep is all you need!

DIY | COMMAND CENTRAL CABINET

Repurpose a small cabinet or dresser (or even the inside of a kitchen cabinet or linen closet) to create a stylish landing spot for important entryway necessities.

Here's a handy list of tips and ideas to make over your own DIY Command Central cabinet:

+ Adhesive or other shallow hooks can be installed inside a cabinet door to organize extra keys and even a flashlight for power outages.

+ Clip up an easy-to-grab list of emergency phone numbers (or use a magnetic board).

+ Put peel-and-stick cork squares on the inside of a cabinet door for keeping important household notes organized. (Add a note with your Wi-Fi password.)

+ Labeled trays on shelves corral family paperwork or incoming or outgoing mail.

+ Bins can hold gadgets or personal belongings.

+ Add a babysitter or dogsitter notebook with important instructions to leave with anyone caring for your kids or pets.

+ Design an electronic charging station in a drawer or cubby (drill a hole through the back of a cabinet for the cords) to house all those gadgets and battery chargers.

+ Set up a hospitality notebook filled with favorite restaurants and shopping destinations for guests.

7 | MAKE A MAIL SORTING STATION

Some of the craziest clutter in the entryway is caused by mail—from bills to junk mail to magazines to important correspondence. It's easy to keep adding to a pile or overflow a basket or tray with paper, which also makes it easy to miss payments or misplace documents.

No matter how much entry space you have, it's easy to designate a drop zone or command center system for organizing paper near the front door.

+ Wire baskets mounted on the walls make a cute and rustic mail station. Consider using several baskets: an "in" basket and an "out" basket, or perhaps a separate basket for each member of the family.

+ An old-fashioned wooden mail sorter provides room for incoming and outgoing mail, stamps, envelopes, note cards (perfect for dashing off quick thank-you letters), and pens.

+ Add file folders to your mail station for increased organization.

+ Use built-in shelves, bookcases, or flat surfaces, such as the top of a piano if you don't have an entry table or separate entry space.

+ Hang a clipboard on the wall for correspondence and bills that need your immediate attention.

+ Buckets or decorative tin pails work well on flat surfaces. You can find fun, colorful patterns and designs.

+ Important school papers and other documents can be included in your mail station. Include any items that tend to get scattered around the house or lost in a desk drawer or backpack.

+ A big basket for mail gives you a start on the organizing process. It's a simple solution to disorganized piles, and you can get more detailed later on if you need to.

Living Spaces

MAKE YOUR
LIVING AREA LOVABLE

Perhaps no room causes as much organization confusion as the living room. It's often hard to assess our needs in this space. Maybe you've been led to believe that every home needs a formal living room, so you've created just that, but then you find you don't use it. Perhaps this space sits unused, yet the rest of your house doesn't have enough space to accommodate your needs. Or maybe your living room has morphed into a catchall of activity, but it's so chock-full of stuff that nobody can actually relax or accomplish much of anything in there.

Give yourself permission to repurpose this space in a way that works for your family. Make it attractive so you'll be drawn to enjoy it, but practical and sensible enough to be useful for this season of life. A living room doesn't have to be fancy, and it shouldn't be just wasted space. Make this a room you can actually live in.

Set up your living room to be organized and used for what you truly need and love. Feel free to change things up as your needs change. Surround yourself with things that matter now. Decorate with items that put a smile on your face. Organize with fun, communication, and connection in mind. Above all, your living space is for *you*. Make it your own, make it work for you, and make it work for your family.

8 | MAKE MEMORIES

Do you long to gather some friends together to start a book club or other group? Do your kids need a good hangout space for their friends—or do you need hangout space of your own for when friends or neighbors stop by? Do you dream of family fun nights?

When you're organizing your living space, focus on the word *living*. What kind of memories do you want to make? What will bring laughter to your home? What kind of environment will foster long conversations and sharing?

+ If you dream of family game nights around a real board game, stop dreaming and clear out that armoire or those cluttered shelves in your living room and create an organized space for family games. Donate any games you haven't played in forever and keep only your favorites. You can also swap games with friends to determine if you really want to own them (or just keep a lending library going).

+ People stay where they feel comfortable. Cozy couches and chairs need to be cleared of stuff before people will consider making themselves at home. Also, concentrate on eliminating the clutter from coffee tables or end tables. And sometimes a soft rug (again, free of stuff!) is the best place for a casual hangout.

+ Don't feel that you need to have a perfectly picked-up living room. Too pristine can sometimes be as unsettling as too messy. If guests feel uncomfortable sitting in your space, they won't stay long. Scattered books, family photos, a game in progress on an ottoman, fresh flowers from the garden, or some knitting in a basket by the sofa all say, "We live here. We have fun here. We make memories here."

9 | QUESTION EVERYTHING

Look at what has been hanging on the walls of your living room or sitting on a table or in a cabinet for seemingly forever. What is the story of that item? If you rarely use it, or if it doesn't have a good story that means something to you, let it go! Most things can be easily and affordably replaced if you find you truly do need them later. Better to let go and have to replace something than to hang on to an excessive amount of stuff you may never use again. Chances are, the more you keep, the less you use. Let it go and feel your stress go too.

The process of decluttering can be strangely addicting, and it's easy to move on from that point.

Reset your space back to its original state. It may sound a little extreme, but clearing absolutely everything out of your living room might give you a new vision for how to make the most of your valuable space.

Surround yourself with favorite mementos and objects that remind you of family and friends. You don't have to be surrounded by empty surfaces and barren bookshelves. A manageable number of happy things you love will breathe life and soul into your living room. The less you keep, the more you appreciate what really matters.

Resist becoming emotionally attached to too much stuff. Before you bring an item into your living room, ask yourself, *Do I really enjoy it? Is it a charming addition or just additional clutter to dust around? Is it functional? Do I have a distinct place and purpose for it?* When in doubt, it's better to keep less than to try to style, clean, and organize excess.

Imagine yourself as a gallery curator who changes up the collection somewhat frequently when displaying kids' art or even your accessories. Display a rotating collection of art on a doorway or inspiration wire. Or set aside wall space for the latest masterpieces. (The same method works well for photos.) Challenge yourself to keep only a few accessories or rotate in your favorites. Too much will tend to turn to clutter.

Discover a balance of things that works for you as you bring items in and out of your living space. You'll know you've added too much if the room starts to feel overwhelming for *your* personal taste. Less is more when it comes to being organized, so opt for more function and style with less.

10 | IDENTIFY YOUR FAMILY/ PERSONAL STYLE

When you're assessing your living room, it's important to take a good, hard look at where you're at in life. Does the space match your current season? Do you need to add in some kid-friendly items, or do you need to put away things everyone has outgrown? This can be an overwhelming—and sometimes emotional—process, but it's one that always has a positive outcome.

1. After you've done the initial decluttering to remove unnecessary items, look around and see how much more inviting your space is with clear surfaces and uncluttered corners!

2. Do you have unused furniture in this room that might contribute to an overly crowded or cluttered ambience? When a room has too many unnecessary pieces of furniture, there isn't breathing room to relax or enjoy gathering in that space. What could be relocated or rearranged to streamline and update your living room? Take some time to better utilize this space.

3. Things you collect—books, movie tickets, postcards, art from travels, quotes that mean something special to you—can be fun to display. If the items are sentimental and fit your sense of style, by all means show them off. They're terrific conversation starters, plus they make you smile. Get mementos out of storage and turn what you love into meaningful art.

4. Assess the activities that take place—or that you wish would take place—in your living area. Do you need more space for sitting down and having lingering conversations? Or does the floor need to be clear for games and active play? Take a realistic look at the needs of those who live in, as well as frequently visit, your home, and make decisions based on your current reality.

5. Just as there are many different personality types, there are various ways to organize. If a comfortable amount of meaningful clutter makes you happy, embrace it. If you breathe more easily in sparse, clean spaces, love that look. Remember, your living room isn't a showplace. It's a place for you and others to enjoy.

11 | REPURPOSE YOUR SPACE IF NECESSARY

Do you actually *use* a formal living area, or would that room be better repurposed as an alternative space? Depending on the size of your home and the needs of those who occupy it, you might rethink using the space in a way that better suits your family.

Think *purpose*. What is important to you? What are your family's current interests? What do you wish you had more room to do?

Be flexible. Use creativity. You can combine interests to create a unique, one-of-a-kind room where family and friends are certain to gather, relax, and become inspired. How could you better organize the living space you have to make room for valued activities?

Divide your room into activity zones to organize the space for multiple uses, or even repurpose a room for your unique needs.

+ If you love books and art, turn a corner of your space into a library/gallery/art room.

+ Performing families could take advantage of an extra room to have a music and movie area.

+ You could combine a home office with a homeschool area.

Is your space limited or still feeling too cramped for everything you need? Make choices for what can stay and what should be relocated to a different spot. If you play board games more than you read, store the books elsewhere and put the games front and center. Kids constantly begging for read-aloud time? Move out the decorative items and replace them with children's literature. Need space to stretch and unwind? Eliminate an unused chair and create an exercise corner. If you love it, you need to make room for it!

AFTER

BEFORE

12 | SET SOME GOALS

As you're organizing your main living space, have your ideal end result in mind. Set reasonable goals in words and pictures. Put your organizing plan into motion with an eye toward an achievable goal. This will help you stay on track and not become overwhelmed.

ESTABLISH YOUR LIVING ROOM'S PURPOSE

How do you want to use this room? As a place for rejuvenation? A place to unwind with family? A place to welcome new friends? Defining the purposes of your home will help you set appropriate goals for organizing your space.

LOOK FOR NEW IDEAS

Peruse magazines, Pinterest, and blogs for specific organizing ideas that will work for your space. Look for simple solutions to organize your bookshelves, create more open space by rearranging furniture, and display your treasures in a clutter-free, aesthetically pleasing way.

GATHER INSPIRATION PHOTOS

Look at your favorite inspiration room. Notice how much stuff is pictured and compare that to your own room. I know it's tempting to simply dismiss the inspiration room as unachievable perfection when there is not a dirty dish or pile of laundry in sight. As you rethink how you use your space, declutter, and organize your necessities, your home can look just as neat and clutter-free as your favorite inspiration room (after a quick tidying up, of course). What storage pieces are in your inspiration room? How could you creatively incorporate similar functional places for everything you need in your living space?

BE CREATIVE WITH WHAT YOU HAVE

While it may feel overwhelming to look at your growing wish list of organizers or furniture you want for your living room (especially as you surf Pinterest boards!), remember that it's often more cost effective to find creative solutions or use what you have in a different way.

Paint gives new life to just about any piece of furniture. Wallpaper (or giftwrap) on the backs of cabinets or surfaces of boxes can add personality to a humdrum piece. Keep your eye out at thrift shops and yard sales for unique pieces that could be used to streamline or organize your home.

Allow the space to evolve naturally—and enjoy the activity!

13 | MAKE ROOM FOR WHAT YOU LOVE

Homes are most beautiful when they are fully lived in and loved on, don't you think? Let's face it, living rooms will get messy (if we actually live there, that is). The day's homework or projects might be scattered on the coffee table. Kid and dog toys might be all over the floor, signs of a happy and active family. Give yourself grace for the everyday mess that tends to multiply in well-loved spaces.

But if you want to have room for the things you truly love, your space will need to be regularly cleared of the things you are *not* using or currently enjoying. Surfaces covered with last week's dishes and months of unopened junk mail, and floors covered with dirty laundry or clutter, don't allow room for living well today. Remove or put away what is no longer needed in that space, making room for new projects and experiences!

Start organizing this space by assessing what types of messes you have in the living room at the end of every day. Papers? Books? Art or hobbies? Electronics? Schoolwork? Dinner dishes? Clothes? Coats? Blankets? Laundry?

Set up a plan to resolve each problem with a practical solution.

+ A closed storage piece can streamline the look of a room while providing a location for craft supplies.

+ A stack of lidded baskets could stash your handcrafts and hobbies so you can bring them out as needed and put them away with ease.

+ Books and magazines look better organized in trays or baskets instead of piled in haphazard stacks.

+ Library books are best kept in their own storage container. Designating a separate basket or shelf for library items makes them easy to locate when they're due. Best way to avoid stress and fines.

+ Remotes and devices can live in their own tray, basket, or wood box too.

+ Cords can be tamed with special cord-keeping devices.

+ Flat surfaces should stay as clutter-free as possible. Resist the urge to fill an empty space. In a room full of activity that can easily become cluttered, margins and breathing room are even more important.

+ Furniture with hidden storage is ideal for media, games, magazines, and hobbies (such as yarn and needles for knitting). Keep your eye out for benches and ottomans that provide extra seating as well as storage.

+ A storage ottoman makes the perfect rotating toy box for little ones. Change up the toy selection by month or season.

+ Current newspapers and magazines can be corralled in a big basket, which is way more organized than pages scattered everywhere.

+ Need more storage space? The best way to create additional storage space is to get rid of what you don't use in that space to make room for what you do use.

14 | STRIKE A HAPPY MEDIUM

What inspires you to be happy at home? What brings you peace? What brings laughter into your living room? Design and organize your home to reflect the personality of your family. Accessories and mementos can bring laughter or joy, but stuff that isn't loved and cared for becomes clutter.

Give yourself small goals. Even if you're tempted, you don't have to get rid of everything or start redecorating from scratch. That might be unrealistic—and expensive! When you eliminate what you don't need or love, the pieces that are keepers really pop. If you have too many accessories, reduce them by 50 percent. If your living room still looks cluttered, go through again and remove another 25 percent. Keep going until you strike the perfect balance and have pared things down to what feels right to you.

Surround yourself with what you love, but not too much! My family happens to love books and decor. But if our storage areas are full of things we love, if we can't find what we are looking for, or if what we have is always dusty and rarely used, we know it's time to let some of what we love go. Send treasures off to be enjoyed by a new family. Letting go can be an unexpected blessing to both of you.

🔖 **Tip:** Make it a family rule to put personal belongings away before bedtime. Look around the room to see what's out of place and do a quick tidy up to put the room back together again for the next day. It's much easier to restore order to a space each evening than it is to let the messes pile up for weeks.

Kitchen & Dining Room

Kitchen & Dining Room

PREPARING FOR COOKING AND CONNECTION

When your cabinets are sticky and your drawers are full of crumbs, or you can't find room for your everyday necessities because every cabinet and drawer is filled to the brim, working in the kitchen can be a frustrating experience.

The never-ending cycle of meal prepping and cleanup in a kitchen can cause even type A personalities to throw in the towel on cleaning and organization and say, "Forget it! I give up. It's just going to get messy again in a few hours!"

Same with the dining room. Kids do homework there. Parents pay bills. Little ones get going on elaborate craft projects. Often, there's hardly any space left to actually set down plates and glasses for a meal. Piles grow and multiply, and meals are shifted elsewhere or simply eaten on the go.

It may take a bit of time, but you can apply the same simple organizing methods to your kitchen and dining areas. Start by arranging your area into task zones. Take a realistic look at what you need to accomplish and the items you need to do it. Figure out workable solutions for storage. As always, get rid of what you never use to free up space for your necessities. And put an easy-to-implement routine into place.

Once you've taken these simple steps, you'll feel so much more content with your kitchen and family-friendly dining area. These areas are the heart of the home, where you nourish body and soul. They're worth the effort to make them feel as inviting and functional as possible.

15

POWER CLEAN AND ESTABLISH A ROUTINE

Just a few steps performed on a regular basis help you get your kitchen in shape so you can get on with the fun stuff.

Ready for a power clean? Let's do this.

1. Unload the dishwasher and put away all clean dishes. Load the dishwasher with all dirty dishes. Clean all pots and pans and wash anything that needs to be hand-washed until you have an empty sink.

2. Clean the stovetop.

3. Wipe down appliances, blenders, microwaves, and toaster ovens. Run soapy water through your blender to clean it. Polish up cabinets to clear fingerprints or smudges.

4. Clear and wipe off all counters.

5. Take out the garbage.

6. Sweep the floors and then mop to shine them up.

7. Deep clean your sink. (For my white, cast-iron sink, I use Bon Ami or baking soda and Castile soap to make my own cleaning paste. Check with your sink manufacturer for how to safely clean yours.) Polish the faucet.

8. Enjoy the daily tidying ritual. Invest in pretty dish towels (free up space in a drawer by storing towels in a wire basket by the sink), and set a brand-new dish-scrubbing brush in a pitcher or jar.

Tip: A cleaner home is a healthier home too! Pare down the harsh and harmful chemicals under your sink. Stick to baking soda, vinegar, or a few plant-based products for the health of family and friends. You can add scent and naturally deodorize with pure essential oils. Try basil, lavender, lemon, or geranium to make your kitchen smell like a garden. And with fewer products under the sink, you'll have even more room for other things you need.

16 | ARRANGE AREAS INTO TASK ZONES

Do you ever experience avalanches in your kitchen? Is it hard to find room for dishes or food in your cabinets because they're already filled to the brim? Does preparing meals take forever because it's impossible to find your ingredients?

No matter what size kitchen you have, it's helpful to arrange the space according to the tasks you need to perform in it. Don't worry about perfection here. While drawer dividers and labels can be attractive and handy, it's best to start simply. Silverware or gadgets tossed in drawers works just fine—as long as they're the correct drawers. When everything is within easy access, kitchen work is just more efficient!

Figure out what zones your kitchen might need and how small areas might be best utilized.

+ A baking zone (muffin tins and baking dishes, utensils, mixing bowls)

+ A cooking zone (pots and pans with lids, casserole/baking dishes, serving dishes and bowls, colanders and strainers, cooking utensils, herbs and spices, cooking oils)

+ A food storage zone (glass or plastic storage containers, labeling supplies)

+ An everyday dishes zone (dinner plates, saucers, cups, bowls)

+ A coffee or tea zone (coffee, tea bags, mugs, stirrers, flavored syrups, sweeteners)

+ A chopping zone (cutting boards, knives, vegetable peeler, other gadgets)

+ A cleanup zone (hand soap, dish soap, dishwasher detergent, scrubber, dish towels, dish drainer, compost and recycling containers)

17 | DEAL WITH THE DISHES

While clean dishes make me smile, dirty dishes make me downright cranky. And a sink filled with dirty, smelly dishes makes it easy to say, "Forget cooking dinner tonight! Let's go out." (Maybe three nights in a row?) The main mess in a kitchen usually involves a pileup of dirty dishes. So what can we do? We can deal with them—right now!

Load the dishwasher and run it at night. Do it every night. Even when you're tired. Waking up to a counter piled with dirty dishes is guaranteed to start the day with additional stress and will lead to even more clutter and pileups. Be sure to collect dishes from every room in the house before you run the dishwasher to keep other areas clean too.

Unload the dishwasher every morning. This makes it easy to load dishes in throughout the day while keeping your sink and counter space clear.

Sort silverware before you wash it. This makes unloading the dishwasher a breeze.

Don't stack dirty dishes in the sink. Make it a policy to load them into the dishwasher right away or wash them by hand. The exception: You can soak the super dirty stuff or stack dishes in a bin to keep the sink clear while you're cooking. But tackle those dishes ASAP too!

Wash and rinse as you go. As you cook and bake, do the dishes. When you're waiting for water to boil, wash and dry a few mixing bowls. Reuse dishes and utensils as you go for less mess and easier cleanup at the end.

Open shelving works well for quick cleanup. If you're short on cabinet space, free up additional room with open shelving for everyday plates and bowls. Dishes are easy to put away when you can just place them on open shelves. I like an all-white dish theme for open shelves. Even if the pieces don't match, the white gives a simple, clean, and coordinated look.

Motivate yourself. Make the most of time spent doing dishes. Light a favorite candle. Listen to music or a podcast. Reward yourself with a little treat when your kitchen chores are completed.

18 | FIGURE OUT FOOD STORAGE AND ORGANIZATION

+ Create zones for organizing your stored food: snacks, breakfast items, pastas, sauces, bulk foods, canned goods, soups, etc.

+ Collect baskets, wire or metal bins, and colorful crates or metal buckets over time for cupboard and pantry storage. Cute and functional, these keep you organized while adding a bit of decorative pop.

+ It's impossible to organize clutter. Bite the bullet and toss any food that is expired or that you know your family won't eat.

+ Store bulk items, such as grains, beans, and oatmeal, in large glass jars. Buy in bulk to save money and store what's not in the jars in bags hidden inside decorative crates, buckets, or baskets. Simply refill your jars as needed.

+ Use chalkboard labels to identify anything that's not easily visible. These look adorable affixed to baskets, crates, or other containers. If it's labeled, it's likely to be used.

+ Store paper plates, plastic utensils, and other seldom-used items in baskets up and away from the things you grab on a more frequent basis.

+ Make sure snacks are easily visible in a wire crate or basket. This ensures they'll be eaten before they become stale. Keep things tidy and save money at the same time.

+ Put small, preprepared containers in the fridge to organize cold lunch items, snacks, drinks, veggies, and fruit to take to school or work.

+ Your goal should be the least complicated system that works for you. Everyone organizes on different levels. Go with what works for your household and stick to your system!

19 | CREATE MORE SPACE IN YOUR KITCHEN

No matter the size of our kitchens, they always seem to be a little short on space. And no longer are they equipped with just a few appliances, such as a dishwasher, stove, and oven. Add to the mix microwaves, blenders, stand mixers, food processors, coffeemakers, rice cookers, food dehydrators...all designed to make our life simpler, but each one takes up valuable space in our cabinets! That's where paring down to necessities and making the most of your storage makes sense. You might not be able to add square footage or counter space, but you *can* be smart with the space you have.

+ Assess what small appliances you use on a regular basis. You may be able to streamline a few to one appliance that is more multifunctional. You'll likely discover that you really don't use all of your small appliances, so pare down to only the gadgets you can't live without.

+ Add a wall-mounted magnetic knife holder to free up drawer or counter space.

+ Save cupboard space by adding a hanging pot rack or hooks on the wall for frequently used pots.

+ Use stackable nesting bowls and measuring cups to best utilize drawer or cupboard areas. Items that don't nest take up excess space.

+ Add a rolling island or kitchen cart with a drop-leaf surface to expand counter space. Attach hooks or a towel rod to the side for additional storage.

+ Utilize the backs of cupboards by adding over-the-cupboard organizers, painting them with chalkboard paint for grocery lists, or posting a corkboard to pin recipes. Attach magnetic boards and magnetized spice holders to cabinet doors.

+ Hang open shelves in the kitchen or pantry to make the most of your kitchen's available vertical spaces.

+ Organize the area below the sink for better efficiency. Add hooks, rolling storage drawers, risers, bins, or even a lazy Susan to maximize the space. Try a tension rod to hang cleaning bottles or a towel bar for garbage bags.

+ Place a crock by the stove to hold your most-used kitchen utensils to free up drawer space.

+ Add baskets in the empty spaces above your cabinets to keep items you use less often, such as turkey pans and holiday-themed cookie cutters.

+ Add a hanging wall file organizer with slots to the inside of your cabinet to hold pan lids.

+ Add a lazy Susan for canned goods and spices.

+ Put risers inside the kitchen cabinets as needed to optimize space.

DIY | UNDER THE KITCHEN SINK

The space under your sink is often underutilized or overstuffed. Take some time to transform that valuable real estate into a space with purpose and function. Here are six simple steps to reorganize the space under your sink:

1. Clear out everything so you start with an empty cabinet.

2. Wipe down and clean out the space.

3. Assess what products or items need to be kept under the sink.

4. Set up a drawer system or add risers in the cabinet to add additional storage.

5. Adhere self-adhesive hooks and containers to vertical surfaces (such as the cabinet doors) to conveniently corral small items, such as brushes and sponges.

6. Use containers (baskets or pails work great!) to organize supplies, such as garbage bags, towels, or other necessities. If you have room, add a lazy Susan for spray bottles and cleaning supplies.

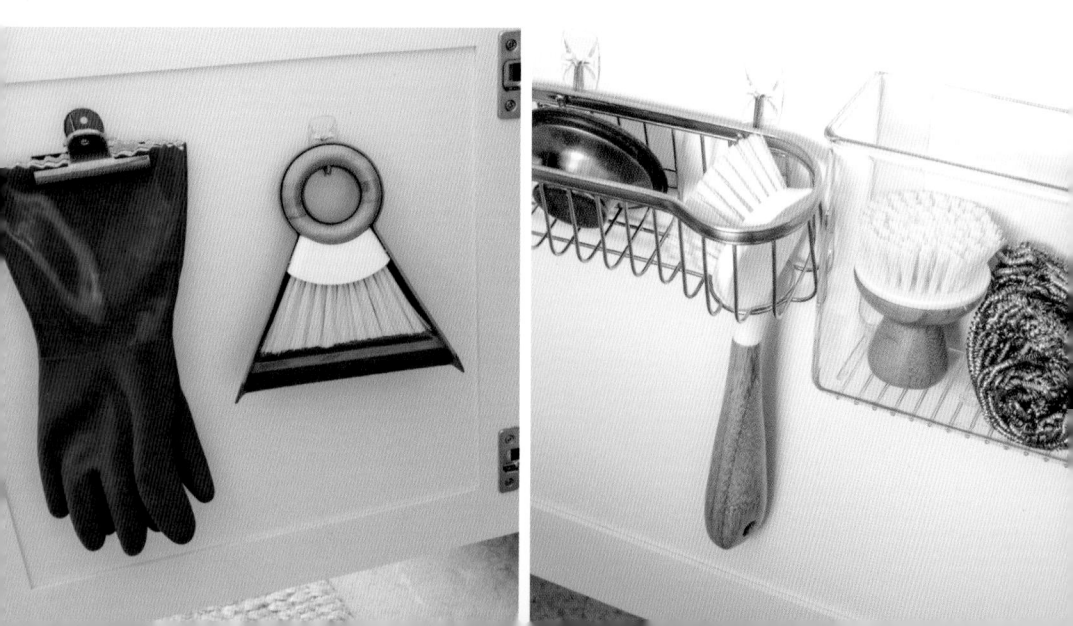

20 | DELIGHT IN YOUR DINING AREA

Flat surfaces are where we tend to dump and pile, and the largest flat surface in your home is most likely your dining room table. Quick—take a peek and see what's currently residing there. Homework? Dirty dishes? Stacks of mail? Toys or packages? Laundry? It's easy to use your dining room as a storage area for a random assortment of things, but you can also decide to make it a place to nurture people and create memorable experiences.

1. Does all the clutter on your dining room table actually belong somewhere else in the house? Gather it all up in a big basket and return the items to their rightful places. Declare your dining table a clutter-free zone! Anything that is brought to the table should be taken away when the activity is completed or by mealtime.

2. See your table as a sacred family gathering space where you offer nourishment to those you love. Clearing the clutter, wiping down the table, and sweeping the floor as you prepare the table for the next meal can become a soothing ritual every day rather than an ongoing annoyance.

3. A buffet, shelves, or other furniture in the dining room doesn't have to be only for dishes. It can hold anything you regularly use at the table, such as coloring books and crayons, a radio, books and projects, art supplies, a container of pens and pencils for doing homework, or a bill-paying basket.

4. Keep something nice on the table at all times, such as a mason jar of fresh flowers or a pretty tablecloth to discourage clutter.

5. Gather items that you can bring out when you want to set up a special meal for family and when entertaining friends. Find cloth napkins in fun patterns or make them out of fabric. Include a set of pretty drinking glasses. Collect dessert or salad plates to dress up your everyday dishes. Gather unscented, colored candles and unique candlesticks (don't forget birthday candles!). Have these items well organized and easily accessible in a basket, dresser, or small cabinet for a spontaneous special meal.

21 | SIMPLIFY MEALTIMES

Do you find yourself running to the grocery store five times a week (sometimes it feels like five times a day)? Are you constantly wondering what to make for dinner? Do you have a fridge full of food but nothing to eat? After you've organized your kitchen, it's time to organize your meal planning.

+ Make a list of five go-to meals that your family loves and are easy to prepare in a hurry. Post your standard meal list inside a cupboard. Next, write out a list of pantry items and fresh food needed to make those meals and keep a copy in your wallet or with your shopping list. Take a photo of the list if it's easier to locate on the go. Each week, assess what you have from the list and replenish when you go shopping so you always have at least five meal options on hand for nights when you are too tired or busy to make something new.

+ Always, always try to plan ahead. At first it may seem like more work, but planning always saves you time in the end.

+ Plan to grocery shop just once a week instead of giving it your first thought at six p.m. and then running out feeling frazzled as you try to decide what to prepare. If you chop and prep the week's veggies on Sunday afternoon, you'll save time later as well as eat more vegetables and less junk.

+ Prep and plan breakfasts and lunches the day before. You can create hundreds of versions of overnight oatmeal, and sandwiches and protein-filled salads make great go-to lunches. Thinking one step ahead will save you stress and frustration the following morning.

Master Bedroom

Master Bedroom

REORDER AND REFRESH
YOUR RELAXATION SPACE

The master bedroom is often the last room we consider organizing because it's usually not on display for others to see. We can close the door when guests arrive, and nobody will think any less of us. (And let's be real. Sometimes we keep the door closed because, in our mad dash to tidy up, we toss all the extra stuff in the master bedroom!)

It's time to rethink this. We spend a lot of time in a bedroom. Never mind that the majority of that time is spent sleeping. Actually, scratch that. *Consider* that the majority of that time is spent sleeping—and that a good night's sleep is the key to an energy-filled, productive day. The last thing you need to feel before crawling into bed is chaos and tension.

Your bedroom should be a relaxing, restful retreat. A few moments spent sipping a cup of chamomile tea and reading a few pages of a book before you turn out the lights work wonders for calming your mind and preparing your body to rejuvenate. Even if you have a crazy-busy day ahead of you, jam-packed with meetings and deadlines and activities and appointments, your bedroom disorganization doesn't have to contribute to the stress of the day.

From paring down the items on the bedside table to editing your wardrobe, in this section you'll gain simple organizing tools to bring calm and relaxation into your bedroom—and into your life.

22 | DISCOVER THE DOMINO EFFECT

There's this thing called the *domino effect*. Once you take the first step (or knock down the first domino), it becomes easier and more motivating to do the next thing, especially as you see the rewards of your efforts. This is true for work and exercise and personal growth. It's also true for cleaning and organizing!

Once you begin to tidy your bedroom, you'll want to keep the momentum going. Not sure where to start? Choose one of these tasks and continue on...and on...and on.

+ Remove as many items from the room as you can to create a peaceful space.

+ Make your bed in the morning. (You'll be glad you took the time.)

+ Wash sheets, pillowcases, and blankets on a regular basis.

+ Clear off nightstands and tidy them up.

+ Remove clutter from floors.

+ Vacuum carpet or rugs, or sweep and dust hardwood floors.

+ Clean out under the bed.

+ Dust all surfaces, baseboards, lampshades, and window sills.

+ Polish up accessories and lamps.

+ Put away clean laundry.

+ Fluff and line up pillows.

23 | ELIMINATE EXCESS TO MAKE ROOM FOR STYLE

Remember when we talked about stepping in your front entry and seeing it in a new way? Try to do that with the other rooms in your home, such as the master bedroom.

Make your bedroom a peaceful destination. It's worth the decluttering and the extra organizing because you spend so much of your life in this room. Make it a priority for this space to be as orderly and refreshing as possible so you'll look forward to spending time there dressing, relaxing, and dreaming.

Add hooks to the back of your doors. Make it simple to hang a towel, robe, purse, or even your outfit for the day to keep everything off the floor or bed.

Place an attractive laundry hamper in the space where you get dressed.

Add a plant to purify the air and bring natural, clutter-free decor to the space.

Gather all your accessories (scarves, jewelry, bags) and choose what you actually use. Donate or give away what you don't wear anymore, and then hang the rest on hooks or store in beautiful containers. Make your accessories feel like pieces of art in your bedroom or closet. Set up a simple system and a home for each type of accessory.

Simplify your jewelry organizing. No need to go shopping right away for fancy organizers. Necklaces can be hung on the wall with hooks or on a pretty bulletin board with pushpins. Hang earrings from a ribbon on a wall or on a corkboard. Bracelets can find a home on a plate or trinket dish, on hooks, or in a shallow basket.

Pare down your stuff to keep your organizing system simple. You need plenty of space to breathe in the bedroom.

24 | WHIP YOUR WARDROBE INTO SHAPE

Overwhelmed by choices? Offer yourself fewer options in what you wear or keep in your closet, and it will be easier to decide what to wear and quickly get ready for your day. You'll also do less laundry. And you'll have less to buy to coordinate with all the random items you never wear because you no longer keep those random things you don't wear. Less clothing results in a more orderly closet, so tidying up will be a breeze.

Avoid temptation. Limit window shopping (in stores or online) as it will cause you to buy more clothes, shoes, or accessories to deal with or tempt you with more decisions that will need to be made. It's amazing how much less you buy and how much easier your subsequent decisions are when you spend less time shopping.

When in doubt, throw it out. When you're paring down your wardrobe, you don't have time to analyze every possible item. If you haven't worn something in the past year, you probably won't wear it again. Don't think about how much money you spent on it. Donate the item to a worthy cause or a good friend and move on.

Do you already have the item in the same or a different color? Is life better with two nearly identical clothing items, or can you make do with just one?

Choose three items you could easily remove from your closet. These may be items that don't fit well or aren't really your style or color. Put them in a giveaway bag for someone who will feel beautiful in them. If you're feeling inspired, choose three more items...and three more...and three more.

Still feeling indecisive about an item? Choose to let that thing go. If you ever find a new one that you really love and know you'll use, you can replace it. But chances are, you probably won't miss it.

25 | REMEMBER YOUR ROUTINE

The best way to get your day off to a good start is with a simple morning routine that doesn't take too much work yet makes you feel happy and productive from the start.

+ Disorder in the morning is a domino that causes even more disorder by the evening. Simple routines help you wake up energized and ready to tackle the day. You know what you need to do...and you start doing those things automatically once they've become a habit.

+ Let your bed-making ritual be an enjoyable part of your morning. Spritz a linen spray or essential oil blend on your sheets before you pull up the covers. Find special pillows to prop up against your headboard and a beautiful throw to drape across the end of the bed. (If you have pets or kids, find one that is machine washable.)

+ Making your bed and straightening up your bedroom before you leave for the day allow you to return to an orderly, calm space that evening. Even if the best you can do is to quickly straighten out the sheets and blanket and prop up your pillows before you leave the room, you'll feel less frazzled when you return. A peaceful evening is worth a few extra moments at the start of the day.

+ It's important to incorporate enjoyable little rituals into your morning. I have a coffee station all set up with my favorite mugs, a milk foamer, and a French press so I can mindlessly but mindfully indulge in my morning coffee. I might sit for a few moments in silence, relaxing and enjoying the view outside our window. This little ritual is often the nudge that gets me up and out of bed!

+ A few simple habits establish a rhythm of order in a day. My morning routine, which involves quiet time, making my bed, taking a shower, and getting dressed (right down to my makeup, shoes, and even earrings) sets the rest of my day in a positive direction.

+ Morning habits bring more clarity and peace to every day because they are decisions you don't have to make. They are tasks that have already been decided. You just have to follow through.

26 | PUT YOUR CLOSETS AND DRAWERS TO WORK

The first step in the simple organizing of closets and drawers is getting rid of what you don't need. Once you have what works for you, make smart use of your storage space.

+ Develop an eye for order. When you see untidy closets and drawers, take a few moments to group like items and straighten wayward pieces.

+ Picture the organizing style of your favorite boutique clothing shop. The items are folded neatly on the shelves. Everything is within reach, and nothing is stacked too high. You're able to select clothes with ease because they are hung with breathing room between them on attractive matching hangers.

+ Organize your closet (and make getting ready to head out the door easier) by grouping like items. Shirts together, pants together, dresses together. While you can organize by color if that inspires you, items will look especially tidy if each category is grouped by the length of the item.

+ Make a visual note of how much space you have for your hanging items. Choose to only hang in-season clothes you actually wear regularly and are in good condition.

+ If your closet is still stuffed even after paring down items, see if anything currently hanging up could be folded (such as jeans or T-shirts) and stored elsewhere. Likewise, if your drawers are crammed but your closet has extra space, hang up some items.

+ Invest in matching hangers! Count how many hangers you need and only buy that amount. Your closet will look tidier if the hangers are the same style or at least the same color. Buy slim, nonslip hangers whenever possible.

+ Make the shelves in your closet functional (decide how many items you can stack without it being a hassle to get them out) and fold the items carefully so they look tidy. Group purses, shoes, sweaters, and T-shirts.

+ Shoes can be tucked into back-of-the-door or wall shoe pockets, an extra drawer, or an under-the-bed organizer for easy access if you don't have room in your closet. Make a list of organizers or supplies you'll eventually need to make the most of the space you have.

27 | CREATE A COZY NEST

The mood of your sanctuary can be transformed by daily choices. Streamline your bedroom so it feels both calm and cozy. As you declutter, organize, and decorate, make deliberate choices that will inspire you to rest and take comfort in your space. Say yes to what brings order and peace and no to what increases clutter and stress.

TEXTURES OVER TCHOTCHKES
The bedroom should be a place of rest. Move collections and excess decorations. They just collect dust and are visually distracting. Instead, fill your room with touchable textures. Cozy bedding, rugs, and window treatments quiet a room and elevate the sense of comfort.

MINIMALISM OVER MAXIMALISM
Even if you are naturally more of a maximalist when it comes to design preferences, your bedroom might serve you better if you err on the side of minimalism. Excessive furniture, patterns, and belongings may interfere with the mood you need to sleep or retreat from the hectic pace of life. Where could you streamline and simplify your design?

CURATED OVER CHAOTIC
Look at each element in the room as an opportunity to curate a work of art that inspires you. Look at your walls, your furniture, your fabrics. Select each item to enhance the beauty and peacefulness of the overall space.

CLOSED CABINETS OVER OPEN DISPLAY
Even if your intention is to have a tidy bedroom, nightstand tables with open shelving below can be difficult to maintain. Ideally, closets should have doors or curtains to conceal elements inside. If you must have a computer or office in your bedroom, hide reminders of work in drawers or cabinets.

SERENITY OVER STRESS
Guard your bedroom from unnecessary stress by making this space your sanctuary. Make your bed every day and deal with the laundry elsewhere. Perhaps head to the living room to watch the news and instead play soft music when you retreat to the bedroom. Keep the lights low in the evenings to create a calm, peaceful mood.

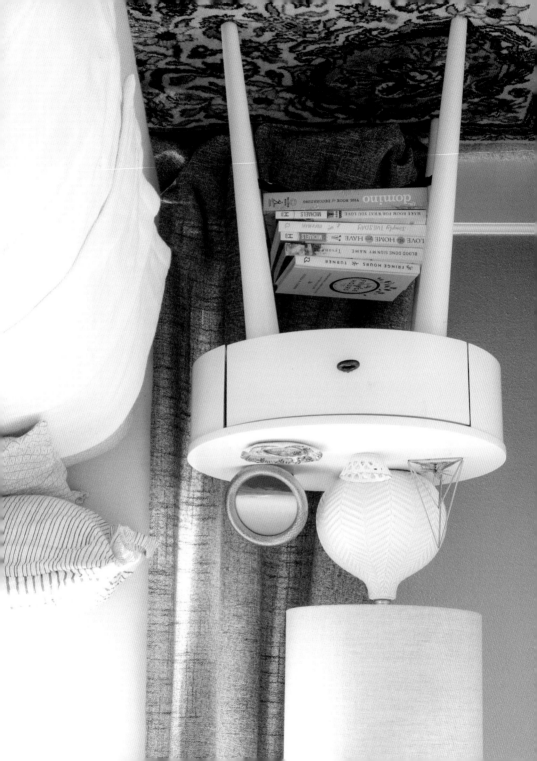

28 | DECLUTTER YOUR DRESSER AND BEDSIDE TABLE

Your bedroom might not have many flat surfaces, but the top of the dresser and the bedside table tend to gather stuff—from electronic gadgets to spare change to random receipts. These clutter piles grow and grow until your bedroom becomes a catchall for junk.

Look at your nightstand. What's on it? Dust the surface and only put back what you actually need—perhaps a lamp, a clock or a charger for your cell phone, and a few favorite books neatly stacked and topped with a decorative candle.

Find cute trays and containers to help create order. You can store chargers, jewelry pieces, or even spare change in these while maintaining order on the flat surfaces.

Clean out the drawers in your dresser and bedside tables. Create space for things that are getting piled on top. If you have a nightstand with an open shelf below, stack a nice grouping of books or add a basket that fills the space. That will reduce the temptation to clutter it up!

Add a vase of fresh flowers to the top of the dresser or nightstand. Every time you change the flowers, take the opportunity to dust, declutter, and clean the rest of the surface.

29 | SIMPLIFY WITH ORGANIC STYLE

Decorating with natural elements makes simple organizing easy. You don't have to store or clean the decorations. At the end of the season—or when they've wilted or faded—into the compost bin or yard debris container they go. Good for you, good for the environment.

SPRING

Daffodils, tulips, and iris

Blue glass vases and mason jars

Blooming branches

Moss and twigs

Wildflower bouquets

SUMMER

Shells in a container of sand

River rocks

Blossoms floated in glass bowls

Bouquets of herbs, such as rosemary and lavender

AUTUMN

Mini pumpkins

Asters, chrysanthemums, and sunflowers

Pinecones and sprigs of evergreen

Leaves and branches

WINTER

Pinecones and mini trees

Branches spray-painted gold

Twigs spray-painted white

Baby's breath and evergreen clippings

Bathrooms

Bathrooms

CREATE A SIMPLE SPA AMBIENCE

While classy bathrooms with marble counters, gorgeous faucets, and beautiful tile make my heart beat a little faster, above all else, clean, uncluttered bathrooms are my favorite. A bathroom sparkling and stocked with fresh towels, toilet paper, soap, and other essentials can almost seem like a brand-new place.

A well-organized bathroom helps you streamline your morning routine. When the bathroom is put together, you feel more put together. Having hair-care items, makeup, and bath supplies simply but attractively ordered and displayed will save you time and sanity. Think pretty yet functional when it comes to storage. Clean and spare. Consider the function of the space—getting yourself ready to go.

The bathroom is a great place to make a shift toward a more natural and healthy lifestyle. Pare down excess and incorporate better quality cleaning and personal products that are good for your body and will make your bathroom feel more luxurious.

And while function is important, don't forget to add a little spa ambience to the bathroom. Sometimes you just need a bubble bath session—or a long, hot shower. Tidy and fresh bathrooms boasting a little charm are a winning combination.

30 | STREAMLINE YOUR CLEANING ROUTINE

Okay, deep breath. Are you ready to give your bathroom a thorough cleaning? You really only have to do this once in a while, and then in between you just maintain. If your bathroom is pretty nasty (and there's no shame in admitting this; it happens to the best—and busiest—of us), don't feel guilty hiring a professional housekeeper to do the job for you. Post this list inside a bathroom cupboard to help you to focus on efficiency.

1. Wash the shower curtain, liner, and any window curtains and blinds.

2. Clean the toilet bowl and polish the top, sides, and toilet base.

3. Scrub the tub or shower.

4. Clean out the medicine cabinet and safely discard old products.

5. Wipe out the drawers.

6. Take out the trash.

7. Rehang the curtains and shower curtain and liner.

8. Clean the mirrors.

9. Polish the counter and sinks and counter accessories.

10. Sweep the floor and mop.

After you've accomplished the big chores, you can maintain the order in five- to ten-minute cleaning bursts. You can start by polishing up the sink in under a minute! Eventually, bathroom cleaning will become second nature, and you'll have a streamlined routine permanently in place.

31 | TRANSFORM THE TOWEL AND TOILETRY SUPPLIES

It's easy for our bathrooms to become overrun with towels and toiletries. It may seem impossible to have 80 million products in the shower and no conditioner, but it happens. And all those towels on the floors and counters—which ones are clean or could have been used again?

+ Pare down your towel stash to only the best of the best (perhaps to simplify, set a goal of just two bath towels per person, two hand towels, and several washcloths). Make a note to invest in a new set if your towels look as if they've seen better days.

+ I like using an all-white color scheme for my towel collection. They always match, and a little bleach keeps them looking fresh. This is also a great way to avoid those bleached-out spots that facial cleansers leave on colored towels.

+ Install extra rods and hooks on the back of the door to maximize your space for hanging and drying towels. It's easier to avoid the temptation of throwing your towel on the floor when it's just as easy to hang it up on a designated hook.

+ Keep track of your towels. Sew on simple colored tabs or ribbons to distinguish whose towel is whose. You can also purchase decorative numbered hooks or stencil numbers above hooks and assign a number to each family member. Bonus: Hanging up the towels helps them dry quickly!

+ Store extra supplies (toilet paper, soap, shampoo, and conditioner) in another location but keep track of what you need to repurchase as you run out. It saves money to buy in bulk, and fewer trips to the store also saves significant time.

+ Do you really need to display decorative items on your bathroom counters and shelves? Attractive containers for items you actually use are decoration enough. A basket filled with colorful bath bombs or a mirrored tray holding a few favorite lotions will give the bathroom that simple spa vibe.

32 | CORRAL SUPPLIES IN CREATIVE CONTAINERS

While it might be tempting to go with a specific decorating theme for your bathroom and shop for various items, the reality is that bathrooms easily become cluttered with extra stuff. Attractive containers for items you actually *use* can serve as decor without the added clutter.

1. Hang a small tray, basket, or shelf near the toilet to hold extra toilet paper, a candle, or a natural air freshener spray.

2. Store such necessities as cotton swabs and cotton balls in a fancy jar. That will add a luxurious touch to simple, everyday items. Bonus: Search for free printable container labels if your jars aren't clear.

3. Paint small wooden crates and use screws to mount them on the walls.

4. Fill a lazy Susan with unique containers that hold items from toothbrushes to sunscreen to hair ties.

5. Use uniform plastic bottles for shower essentials such as shampoo, conditioner, and body wash. Besides looking classy, matching containers also fit better on shower shelves or in a wire shower caddy.

6. Mount hooks on out-of-the-way wall space for hair tools, such as curling irons and straighteners. You can also store these in a metal bin or filing box, which makes it safe to put them away while they're still hot.

7. Set perfume or pretty lotion bottles on a mirrored tray. They will decorate your bathroom and be easily accessible.

8. Stand makeup brushes in a jar for easy access.

9. If you have double sinks with space in between on the counter and need more storage space, add a cute basket to stash your hairbrushes or cosmetics, jars for makeup brushes, attractive bottles for bubble bath, or a tiered shelving unit to hold towels or extra supplies. Group similar items into cute containers, baskets, or jars.

10. Use attractive organizers and dividers to keep makeup, accessories, and toiletries orderly in your drawers. Keep counters clear. Your daily items can be just as accessible out of sight in drawers.

33 | CONSIDER SIMPLIFYING YOUR CLEANING PRODUCTS

Have you taken a good look at your favorite cleaning products lately? A while ago, I did an assessment of the items in my cleaning caddy and realized that many of them were laden with harmful chemicals. Because I wanted to eliminate toxins from my home, I replaced them with options that were healthier for my family and healthier for the environment. The process was actually quite painless. Bonus: I ended up with fewer products to organize and store!

Be diligent about reading labels, but don't freak out. Changing up things can actually simplify your cleaning. Remember the natural-living rule of thumb: It's only truly clean if the products you use are healthy and safe.

Question what you use. Many cleaning products contain toxic chemicals. Research ingredients online or in books to see how "natural" a product is. Also, be careful of some candles and air freshener sprays. Healthier alternatives can be found. (A word of advice: Even products labeled "natural" aren't necessarily good for you.)

Embrace essential oils. Use an essential-oil based diffuser, reeds in a glass bottle, a few drops of essential oil on a cotton ball to make your bathroom smell scrumptious or you can make your own spray bottle room freshener. Just be sure you're using pure essential oils with no artificial ingredients added.

Use lemon juice and baking soda to clean your sink. Simple, effective, and totally nontoxic.

Clean out your drains naturally. Pour one-half cup baking soda down the drain, followed by one-half cup vinegar. After it fizzes, pour six cups hot water down the drain.

Clean your toilet bowls quickly and easily. All you need is one-quarter cup baking soda and one cup vinegar. No need for specialty cleaners.

Pare down cleaning products to just one or two all-purpose cleaners. Combine one-half cup vinegar and one-quarter cup baking soda with one-half gallon water. Spot test on sensitive materials, such as countertops or flooring. Add your favorite essential oil to personalize it!

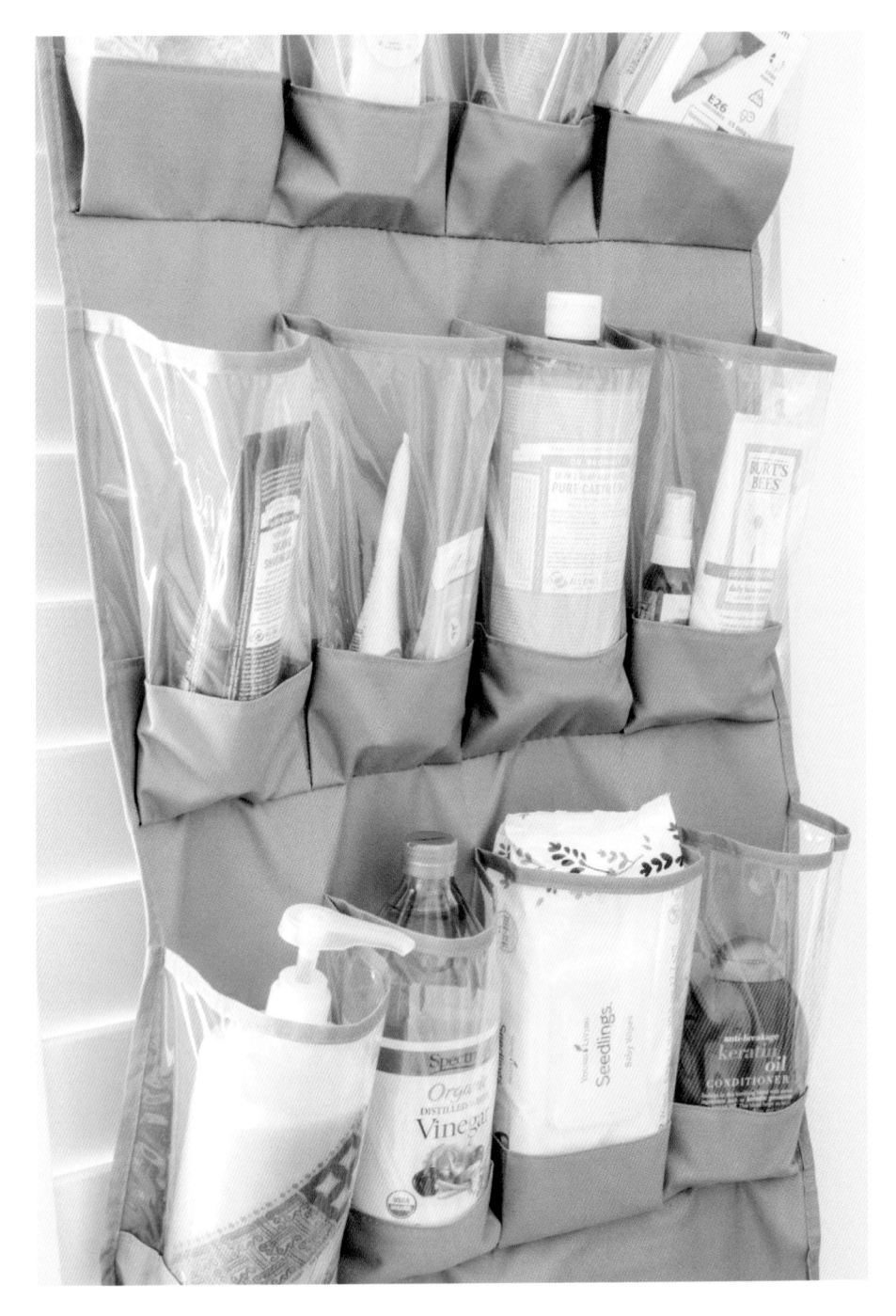

34 | PAMPER WITH A PERSONAL SPA

One of the most productive ways I've found to motivate myself to clean, pare down, and organize a bathroom is to visualize it as though it is my own personal spa.

A day of pampering wouldn't be nearly as inviting if the sinks and counters were covered in soap scum and dried toothpaste. I know I couldn't relax in a spa if it was filled with dirty laundry, trash, or half-empty cosmetic containers.

A bathroom is a destination in your home that deserves a little more care and attention to detail because YOU deserve it. When a bathroom is clean and streamlined, it simplifies daily routines and enhances the whole experience too.

As long as you're committed to the hard work of cleaning and organizing your bathroom, take the opportunity to invest in a few pampering indulgences. Spa accessories can be a positive motivator and a reward for your cleaning efforts.

Invest in spa-like luxuries such as:

+ A long-handled brush for washing your back

+ A hand massager for your neck

+ A luxurious soap or liquid gel

+ A beautiful, fluffy set of clean towels

+ Delicious-smelling soaps. You can even match the scents with the seasons. Lilac and lavender in the spring and summer. Cinnamon and peppermint in the autumn and winter.

If you have the space, place a small stack of your favorite magazines or mystery novels in a basket near the bathtub along with an attractive container of bubble bath to invite yourself to kick back and relax.

Gather a box or drawer of items to pamper guests too, such as a bar soap and body wash, toothbrush and toothpaste, dental floss, shampoo and conditioner, disposable razor and shaving cream, bath towels as well as hand towels and washcloths, a few basic first aid supplies, feminine products, and deodorant.

35 | PARE DOWN BEAUTY PRODUCTS

Products accumulate quickly in the bathroom, but we often reach for just a few favorites. Extra products clutter our space and make us feel disorganized. Take some time to assess what you have and what you actually use.

1. Empty the drawers or any storage containers in the bathroom. Throw away any facial products you don't use or that have expired. Get rid of old or never-used nail polish too.

2. Set aside makeup items you don't use regularly but you think you will be likely to use on special occasions (fancy lipstick or eye shadow, for instance). Put those items in a separate pouch or box that can be placed in a less convenient or visible location. If you find you never end up opening that container, let those items go to make more room for what you actually use.

3. Pare down hair accessories, styling tools, and products to only what you use and love. Look in the shower or tub area and declutter any excess.

4. Group together styling and pampering items by category (hair, face, nails, body, teeth). Gather appropriate containers and organizers. Use what you have to get started. Look around the house for small boxes, saucers, pouches, cosmetic bags, or small bowls. (You can always fancy things up later.) Set up an area, drawer, or basket for each category so everything you need regularly has a home that is convenient and tidy.

36 | LIVE WITH LAUNDRY

Did you know that the average family spends five to seven hours per week in the laundry room? Add to that time spent searching for clean clothes and putting away laundry—that's a lot of time! And a lot of reason to streamline your laundry routine and get organized.

Your home might be blessed with a separate laundry room, but don't worry if your washer and dryer are in your kitchen or another nearby space. Close proximity makes multitasking easy. Fold a load of laundry while you're waiting for water to boil. No matter where it's located, focus on keeping your laundry area clean, tidy, simple, and streamlined.

+ Because laundry is a never-ending chore, make a habit to keep up with it every day. Just doing a load or two a day beats spending all Saturday at the washer and dryer. Save your weekends for something fun!

+ If you need a little more organization, break down your laundry tasks into a more specific daily schedule. Here's an example:

MONDAY	towels and whites
TUESDAY	darks and jeans
WEDNESDAY	delicates, shower curtains, and bath rugs
THURSDAY	family's sheets
FRIDAY	master bedroom sheets and towels

+ Complete the entire task: wash, dry, fold or hang, and put away. Don't add extra steps, such as piling clothes first on the sofa and then putting the clothes in the laundry baskets, where they sit for a day or two before finally making it to the appropriate room, or tossing them on the floor to fold later and then having to rewash because they've been on the floor all week.

+ Keep extra supplies of detergent available so you don't run out (which can slow down your efficiency!).

+ Hang a rod you can use as a drying rack or a place to put clothes to avoid wrinkles as you pull them out of the dryer. You may never need an ironing pile again! Take clothes on hangers straight to closets.

+ Refresh your laundry space. Polish up the washer and dryer and toss out lint. Recycle old detergent containers and put detergent in prettier containers or set them up in an attractive way. A pretty and organized space is so much more inspiring.

+ Hang shoe pockets for preventing clutter in a laundry room. Use them to sort your cleaning rags, trash bags, small vacuum cleaner attachments, and refills for your mop. Fill them with spray bottles (such as stain removers) or use them to hold those stray socks until their mate is found.

+ Sort laundry into three baskets for efficiency (whites, colors, delicates). With a big family, it can be convenient to assign a weekly laundry day for each person's clothing to save time sorting (or to teach children to do their laundry!).

+ Put attractive storage baskets on top of a front loading washer and dryer. (For instance, I have one for delicate/special care items.) Woven baskets can look cute and help prevent piles on the floor. A slender cart might slide next to the washer or dryer for detergents. A wall organizer can make the most of wall space. Make the most of the space you have!

37 | SET UP A WELLNESS STATION

When someone in the household gets a bee sting or a sunburn or a splinter, there's often a mad scramble to find the supplies you need for soothing the situation. Why not organize a wellness station? All you need is a big-enough basket and an assortment of your go-to remedies. You might want to add a first aid book and emergency numbers too. (Special note: If you have young children, please be mindful of keeping certain medications stored out of their reach.)

WELLNESS SUPPLIES

Adhesive tape	Homeopathic medications
Aloe vera gel or lotion	Hot water bottle
Antibiotic ointment	Hydrogen peroxide
Apple cider vinegar	Insect repellant
Arnica gel or cream	Isopropyl alcohol
Bandages	Nail clippers
Bee sting remedies	Nail file
Calendula salve	Scissors
Chapstick	Sunscreen
Coconut oil	Tea tree oil
Epsom salts	Thermometer
Essential oils	Tweezers for splinters
Gauze	Witch hazel
Heating pad	

Kids' Rooms

KEEP UP WITH YOUR GROWING TRIBE

If you have kids, your home is going to have what we like to call a "lived-in" look. And the younger your kids are (and the more kids you have), the more this statement is going to be true. But lived-in doesn't have to mean dirty or messy or completely disorganized. A home with kids can still be a comfortable, welcoming, and cozy place for everyone to enjoy.

Simple organizing isn't just good for you and your home. It's also good for your kids! When you give children the opportunity to appreciate or make do with what they have, you teach them contentment. When you encourage them to sort through their items and choose things to give away, you encourage them to develop a spirit of sharing. When you offer fewer options for clothing and toys, you offer greater freedom to make quick decisions and move on to the things that truly matter.

Like adults, kids can become overwhelmed with excessive choices and belongings. When my kids were still small, I would sometimes offer them one of two choices (both good options). The limitations gave them the opportunity to still have a say in a matter without overwhelming them.

From a very young age, kids can learn orderly habits and develop lifelong skills in keeping their things clean and organized. As they grow, so do their responsibilities. As parents, we can guide this growth and together master the art of simplicity.

38 | HELP ESTABLISH ORDERLY HABITS

It's important to teach our children to live responsibly and to be satisfied with what they have rather than always wanting more, better, and newer things. When you help kids establish orderly habits, you help build lifelong skills for staying organized. But beyond that, you teach them to realize the value of caring for and being grateful for what they do have.

+ Keep the basic shell of the room tasteful, neutral, and timeless. Kids' tastes and favorites seem to change all the time. One minute your daughter may be all about Rapunzel from *Tangled*, and the next she is obsessed with Elsa from *Frozen*. Constantly changing the whole room with the latest trend would be expensive and time-consuming and would set up a spirit of discontentment with what she has. Keeping the shell of the room basic and timeless makes it easy to do minor updates and transform the space as your child's tastes evolve. You can add in plenty of your child's personality or favorites with elements, such as artwork in frames, pillowcases, colors, etc.

+ Kids' rooms don't need a lot of decoration. Children already have many colorful and interesting things they love to play with or display. Adding elaborate decor pieces can make a room feel visually cluttered. Give children space to show off their artwork and school projects.

+ Children need simple organizational systems that are easy to use. For organized storage of smaller toys, use under-the-bed container systems with easy-to-change labels (action heroes, doll clothes, tea party dishes, Legos, toy cars, horses, etc.). Divide toys into categories that are practical and useable.

+ Closed or semi-closed storage bins are a must. Cleaning up kids' rooms can feel like a never-ending task. The ability to toss and hide is priceless. It's fine to display a few prized items on open shelves or on the tops of bookcases and dressers, but limit the feeling of visual chaos by utilizing closed bins or baskets for most items.

+ Use a large toy box to store dress-up clothes or costumes. Inspire kids to use their imagination by making it easy to access their favorite costumes. But don't keep small items in a large toy box. It's too overwhelming, and toys may disappear, never to be found again.

+ Add bookshelves wherever you can, but also remember to keep plenty of floor space open. I like to position a bookshelf close to the bed in order to encourage reading. (Remember to safely bolt to the wall any furniture that could be a tip hazard.)

+ Create a to-do list on a chalkboard. Using chalkboard paint, you can turn just about anything into a writing surface. Kids love to write in chalk, and you can teach them the satisfaction of crossing off completed chores.

+ Once the room is set up with a place for everything, give children cleaning routines to maintain their own belongings. Incorporating a daily ten-minute "cleaning frenzy" into the before-dinner routine gives kids valuable practice in keeping a space organized and in order.

39 | INTRODUCE HOUSEKEEPING ROUTINES EARLY

Here's a motto to live by: *Simple done well is better than complicated never practiced.* If a system is too complex, you feel defeated before you even begin. And when you're teaching kids, that's even truer. Giving kids the skills to stay on top of tasks will give them the tools to succeed in any endeavor. Start young and start simple.

+ Provide age-appropriate routines along with scheduled daily cleanup times to help make maintaining order a lifelong habit.

+ Give everyone their own simple morning routine with household tasks suitable for their age or current needs. Even toddlers can help make beds, dust, or bring laundry to the hamper. Young kids can feed pets, set the table, and fold laundry.

+ Include outdoor chores. Many kids love spending time outside working in the garden, washing cars, and joining in on building projects. They're able to burn energy while learning lifelong skills.

+ Communicate your expectations clearly. For instance, show kids how much space they have available for toys or craft supplies, and tell them they can only keep what fits in that space.

+ Allow them some control. Let children help create labels for storage bins and baskets and make suggestions on how to organize. Their style might be different from yours, but they need to feel some ownership. Eventually, they'll be organizing on their own!

40 | STREAMLINE AND SIMPLIFY KIDS' STUFF

The main problem kids have with keeping their rooms clean? *Too much stuff.* Floors and surfaces covered with books, papers, and toys can overwhelm anyone. While we love giving our children a variety of options and have every intention of implementing the perfect organizational system complete with rotating boxes and bins, the reality is that too much stuff sets you back every time. I promise. You aren't a mean mom if you limit how much stuff they have to make a mess of. You're a good mom when you teach your kids to value what they have and appreciate it as well as selflessly give things away so others can enjoy them.

1. Take a critical look at the toy situation. Do your kids have so many toys within reach that they can't possibly keep them organized? Pare belongings down to only a few things your children can play with without your help and put the rest out of reach for times when you can better supervise them.

2. When my kids were younger, I put limited or even no toys or craft supplies in their bedroom. Separating out most of their toys and crafts to other spaces of the house gave the kids a sense that bedrooms were for sleeping, reading, and quiet play.

3. Don't just tell your kids to clean up their room. That's overwhelming to most kids. Show them that books go on bookshelves, stuffed animals go in their basket, and dirty clothes go in the hamper. Then when it's time to tidy, be specific. Let them know it's time to put the books away on the bookshelf so they can successfully complete the task.

4. Help kids to become orderly people. Give them their own shelves to store special things they like and inspiration boards to be creative.

5. Give them less to put away and less to clean up, and model the value of spending time together enjoying experiences over managing stuff.

6. Teaching kids the value of simplicity and being content with less when they are young will impact them in healthy ways for a lifetime.

41 | ARRANGE AREAS FOR IMAGINATIVE PLAY

With just a little extra thought, you can transform a child's bedroom (or playroom) into a cozy and well-ordered retreat instead of a cavern of chaos. A room crowded with too much stuff basically guarantees a short attention span and a significant amount of frustration. Spend just a little time arranging areas for imaginative play, and watch your child's creativity flourish.

+ Divide the room into separate areas that naturally lend themselves to a certain type of activity. A doll corner, a place to play with costumes, a Lego-and-building zone, a reading nook, a special space to color and draw.

+ Think *function* when you're figuring out the separate spaces. Have zones for sleeping, reading books, and dressing, and set up each one

with what they need. Create a separate zone (in another room or designated spot within their bedroom) for toys, and another for table-type work, such as homework or crafts.

+ Toys and crafts should be organized by category and as simply as possible. Give kids buckets, bins, and baskets to store things in each designated area. Avoid complicated category labels that would be overwhelming for kids to utilize. Kids may be able to toss all of their American Girl clothes into a doll clothing bin, but if they have to separate out the doll's flannel pajamas from her winter jogging outfits, organization might end up being more frustrating than helpful.

+ Less stuff might sound like less fun for the kids, but in reality they will appreciate each toy more and may even be inspired to get a little more creative when they aren't overwhelmed and distracted by many options. Rotate the toys in each area so they can enjoy a variety of fun things and discover new surprises in the form of old favorites that have been put away for a period of time.

42 | CONTROL THE CLOTHING SITUATION

While it may seem impossible to tame the clothing monster, the same organizing principles still apply: Fewer choices and a designated home for everything. Kids grow quickly. They spill food on their clothes and get them muddy. That's natural. But you don't need to be constantly doing laundry all day, every day, or desperately trying to find a pair of pants that fits your child.

Pare down clothes. If your kids have outgrown all their school clothes, it's time to clear out the old. There is no use leaving too-small clothing items in the closet, or they might end up wearing them or being frustrated trying to find things that fit. Go through everything and give away good clothes they have grown out of. Sort through sock and underwear drawers to make sure they're stocked with clean items in the correct sizes and in good condition.

Invest in seasonal storage totes. Have a large plastic tote for each child. Dividing clothes by season (spring/summer and fall/winter) works well. While one season's clothes are in closets and drawers, the next season is waiting in the wings. You can add hand-me-down items to the container that's currently being stored.

Hop on the hand-me-down bandwagon. This is a terrific way to declutter and save money all at the same time. Resist the urge to stock up on end-of-season sales. Growth spurts are unpredictable, and what you purchase brand-new may not fit in six months or a year. Get a hand-me-down cycle going with friends. Kids love it too!

Simplify the socks. When my kids were little, we had the worst time with different colored and patterned socks losing their mates. Instead of wearing mismatched socks each day or spending precious time trying to match up all the different colors and patterns, we simplified things. We decided to just purchase one kind of white, everyday socks that went with everything. Easy solution!

43 | SET UP KIDS FOR SUCCESS IN SCHOOL

Having a well-organized study space and a full range of school supplies allow kids to develop effective study habits, work without distraction, and keep assignments and paperwork in order. All valuable tools for success in school—and life!

+ Kids feel more organized and able to get themselves ready for school if their rooms are cleared out and their belongings are streamlined. Every year kids end up with supplies and books from previous school years. Let them be involved in eliminating what is no longer needed and making space on desks and bookshelves.

+ A designated work space is a must. Start with a clear surface. Toss out any old, worn-out pens and pencils and replace with brand-new ones. Stock drawers or baskets with fresh notebook paper, printer ink, study resources, a stapler and three-hole punch, scissors and tape, and any other supplies they need.

+ Chalkboards, magnetic boards, and clipboards are great for projects, and you can use them to help kids learn to organize their own lists of assignments and deadlines.

+ A simple daily planner works well for when kids start receiving homework in class. As kids move on to upper grades, invest in a more detailed planner. They should have this down before college!

+ Corral homework, backpacks, and sport bags. The annual tradition of a new or cleaned-out backpack makes a great transition for kids to a more scheduled and organized school year. Let your kids clean out their old backpack, or if you are starting fresh, let them help pick out their new one. Get them involved in labeling everything and deciding how to organize their own school supplies and backpacks. (Note: Keep the backpacks cleaned out and maintained on a weekly basis so they retain some semblance of order and you don't lose important assignments or reminders.)

Home Office & Creative Spaces

Home Office & Creative Spaces

BRING ORDER TO WHERE YOU WORK

When you're organizing, here's a simple formula to follow: Less stuff = more time. This is especially true in home offices and creative spaces, where papers, supplies, and chaos tend to multiply. In a matter of months, we can accumulate so much stuff that we can't find what we want, let alone see what we already have.

Making more room for what we want to do in life—and freeing up time and space to actually accomplish things—always has a positive and inspiring outcome, even if the process of letting go can feel overwhelming or impossible. When we're trying to decide what to do with the stuff or space in front of us, it's easier to choose the path of less when we remember that less is really more.

When it comes to our home office and creative spaces, we can bring order to our pursuits—be they business or imagination oriented—when we simplify our organizing methods and pare down things to the essentials. Eliminating excess paper and supplies, setting up systems that make sense, and increasing room for learning and growth put us on the path to an orderly and organized life that is inspiring and satisfying.

Space to work. Space to dream. These are goals worth working toward.

44 | TAKE CONTROL WITH A FAMILY COMMAND CENTER

Have you ever missed an important school event or family gathering? You're not alone. I've forgotten to pick my kids up from school on half days because I didn't pay attention to my calendar. I've missed their orthodontic appointments and sent my kids to school with bed heads on picture day! This is where a family command center would have come to the rescue. I've learned now that I can't live without one.

Don't overcomplicate it. Our command center is a simple magnetic blackboard we use for our most urgent papers. We locate it in the hub of our house so we don't miss the important info posted on it. You can also use a cork bulletin board, a magnetic whiteboard, or even clipboards affixed to the wall.

Keep it current and relevant. Include timely papers, calendars, invitations, to-do lists, and activity and school schedules. Use it only for urgent items that have a deadline, and get in the habit of clearing out old papers weekly. We choose not to include bills to pay. (Those have their own distinct destination.)

Include any supplies you need. As you determine what kind of system works best for your household, add any supplies. If you have a chalkboard command center, store chalk and a chalkboard eraser next to it. Magnetic canisters and cups can hold paper clips and pushpins along with pens and markers. Clips work well to hold paper and calendars. Day-of-the-week clothespins are a nice way to display important weekly reminders.

Have fun with it! You can paint the border of a boring corkboard to match your decor. Search for inexpensive add-ons to make the command center personal. The more attractive it looks, the more you'll be inclined to use it. While you're at it, add a few inspirational quotes and photos for good measure.

45 | ESTABLISH A PLACE FOR EVERYTHING

You might have an entire room devoted to crafting and hobbies, or you might have just a few shelves designated for your favorite pursuits. Some homes come equipped with a separate office or study, and in others the dining room does double duty as a work space. No matter your setup, you can organize your crafting and hobby supplies so they're easy to access and ready to go.

1. Spend as much time decluttering as you need to. If you have a lot of supplies and hobby clutter, pick just one hobby or craft category at a time to declutter and organize. While you're working on this part, be honest about what crafts and projects you have done recently. If you probably won't use it, pass it on to someone who will.

2. As you declutter, group items by category (for crafting supplies, you might have scrapbook paper, glue, glitter, gift wrap, ribbons, yarn, fabric, markers, tape, scissors, etc.). Assess what you have. You may have far more duplicate supplies on hand than you really need.

3. Test the supplies to make sure they all work (such as markers, glue, and pens). Sharpen colored pencils. Throw out anything old, broken, or ripped.

4. Organize office and craft supplies, art prints, and other smaller items in a flat drawer system to keep from losing things in deep drawers.

5. Keep a basket of "to-read" materials. This might be magazine articles, newspapers, or books—anything that will take more than two minutes of your time to read. Check the basket frequently, and pull out reading material when you have a few minutes to spare or when you're waiting for carpool pickup or during kids' activities.

6. Don't forget the details. Lining drawers with pretty paper may sound like a silly luxury when we have too much clutter to even see the paper lining the drawer. But when we get rid of things we don't need and organize what we keep, we find we are effortlessly able to indulge in little details such as happy drawers.

7. First, ask yourself if you will really use all the craft stuff you are about to organize. Take an honest look at your hobbies, goals, and schedule. If organized supplies will enrich your life and inspire you, go for it. But if a newly organized space will be filled with stuff you won't use, you should reconsider. In that case, let most of it go. Pare down to one or two simple crafts with minimal supplies and enjoy them to the full.

46 | ROTATE ITEMS SEASONALLY

Whether it's a season of the year or a season of life, you can set up a system for rotating items in your creative spaces. Better to have a simplified room that is inspiring and usable for you now, than a main living space packed to the brim with supplies for every possible occasion.

+ Contain everything! Be on the lookout for attractive bins, baskets, and boxes to make your creative space more functional. Search antique or thrift shops for vintage containers to add character to your space.

+ Save plastic totes for the things you keep in the garage or attic and rotate seasonally. Label your containers clearly on the sides so that what you need is always easy to find.

+ Transport craft supplies from one area to another with rolling carts.

+ Eliminate the bags. A drawer organizer filled with washi tape looks cuter and is much more user-friendly than a bag stuffed with washi tape and other random supplies.

+ Include a birthday bin with card-making supplies, gift wrap, ribbon, scissors and tape, and perhaps a few party gifts you've found on sale.

+ Rotate seasonal activities! Summer art project supplies—along with idea books—are perfect for those "I'm bored!" moments or overcast days. You can make a big deal of bringing out the summer bin on the first day of vacation.

+ While it can be cost-effective to buy art and craft supplies or holiday decor during after-season sales and store them in the appropriate bins, make sure you don't stock up on what you might not use. Everything we buy takes up space, even if it was on sale.

+ Be willing to give up things. If you've gone a few seasons without using something, you're probably not going to use it in the future. You may have had high hopes that you'd get into soap making when you collected all the supplies years ago, but if you haven't made more than one bar of soap in recent memory, it may be time to acknowledge it's time to pass on the supplies to someone else who will enjoy them.

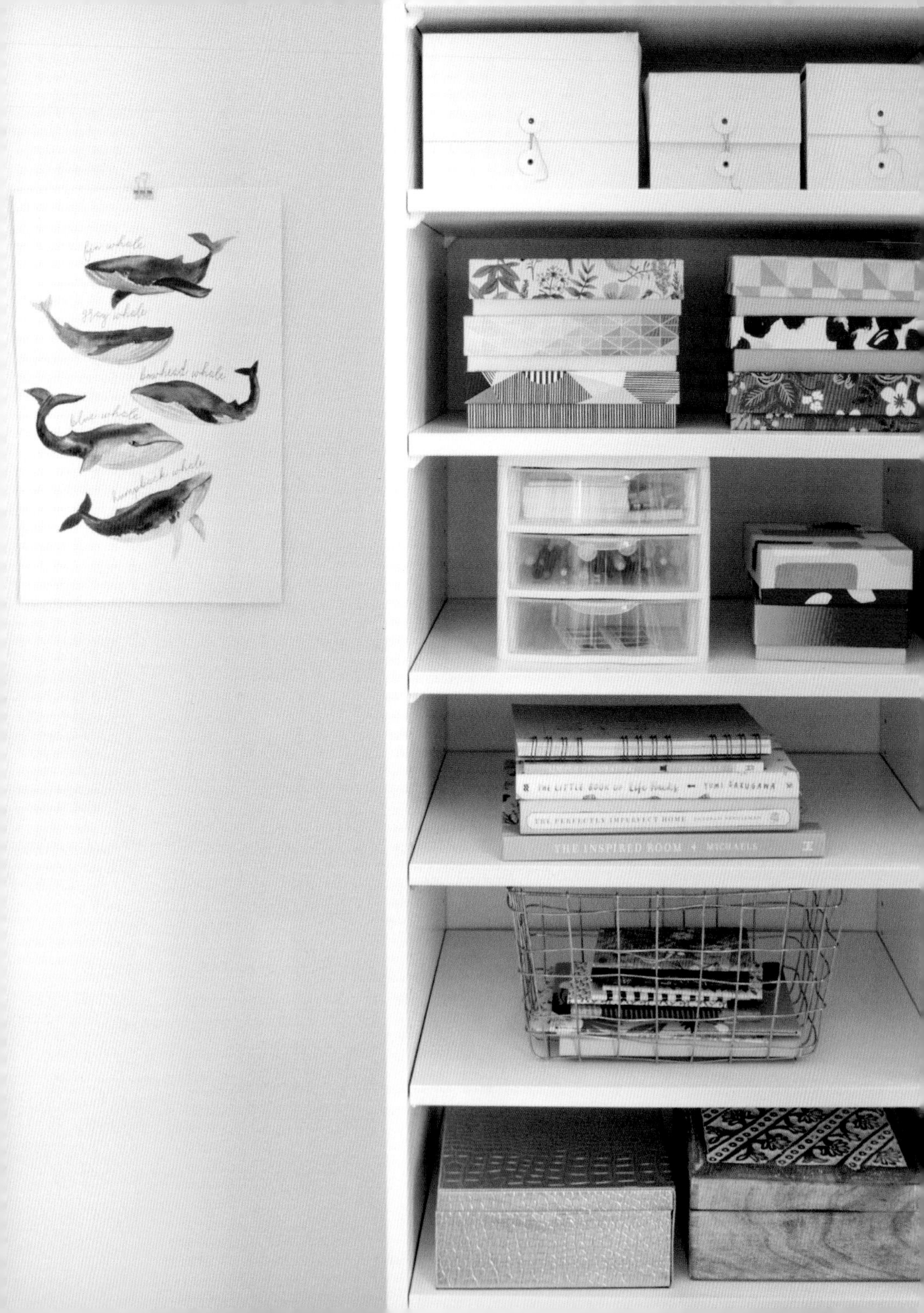
fin whale
gray whale
bowhead whale
blue whale
humpback whale
THE LITTLE BOOK OF Life Hacks YUMI SAKUGAWA
THE PERFECTLY IMPERFECT HOME
THE INSPIRED ROOM MICHAELS

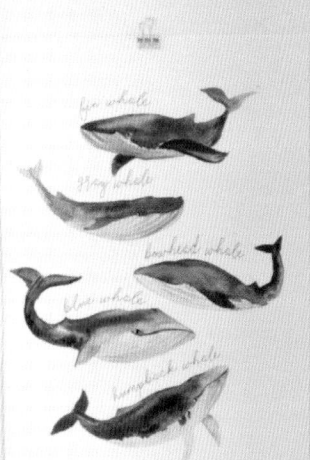

47 | PARE DOWN PAPER CLUTTER

Paper clutter is a common struggle! The less paper in your life, the less you have to sort and manage. Choose paperless systems whenever possible, but beyond that, start with a paper organizing system that is easy to manage and functional rather than complicated and fancy.

Recycle it. As soon as an item comes in to your home, take care of it. If you don't need it, recycle it immediately. Keep a recycling basket handy wherever you tend to handle paper so you never have an excuse to toss items on the counter or floor.

Post it. Post important or time-sensitive stuff (such as concert tickets, sporting event passes, or restaurant coupons you intend to use) in your family command center.

Sort it. We can get inundated with tons of school papers! Sort through these every day and toss what you don't want. We use the super-simple system of taping school papers, lunch menus, and calendars to the back of the pantry door. You could use a cute bulletin board for this purpose too.

Remember it. This is especially important when it comes to bills! I keep a basket for all incoming bills (when paperless billing isn't an option). I open the bill, toss out inserts and envelopes (we pay online), and stick the paper bill in the basket. Twice a month, after I pay the bills, I put the paperwork in a "paid" file drawer, which I recycle at the end of the year.

Shred it. This one is a lot of fun! When I went on a yearlong epic paper decluttering mission, I bought a giant paper shredder and went to town. I shredded the contents of boxes filled with old receipts, bills, school papers, notes, credit cards, statements, and jumbled-up papers of the most random stuff. I recommend this method if you need to get ruthless.

File it. Get a file box or use a file drawer to set up a simple filing system for papers you may need to access in the current year. Label a folder for each category, such as tax documents; insurance documents and medical records; mortgage and car loan documents; important receipts; and warranties. Don't make your filing system too complicated. Only keep on hand what is essential in the current year. Papers you need to save longer (such as tax documents and titles) can be moved to a separate filing system.

48 | SET UP STATIONS FOR SPECIFIC TASKS

Even in a designated home office or creative space, it makes a world of difference to divide the area into special zones for maximum organization and efficiency. (Plus it's fun to decorate these spaces to inspire and delight!)

+ **Brainstorm what you need.** You might need stations for paper and mail, technology, hobbies and crafting, scrapbooking or card-making, homework and reading, or business and office tasks.

+ **Gather your supplies.** For example, in the homework zone you'll want a variety of items within reach, depending on the age of your student—books, pencils, pens, crayons, markers, calculator, bulletin board, stapler, three-hole punch, glue, tape, ruler, dictionary, paper, and highlighters.

+ **Even small areas count.** You can set up an inspiring area in your home prepared with note cards, colored pens, and stamps to send thank-you cards or notes of encouragement to friends. It doesn't take a lot of space, and it brings great rewards. You can set up space in a cabinet you love, in a pretty box with a lid, or even in a brass letter holder on your desk.

+ **Make it fun.** Arrange your area so you get maximum enjoyment while you do a dull task—such as paying the bills. In a corner of a room, I might pull up a comfortable chair to a table. I'll add some luxurious accessories, such as a soft and fluffy throw blanket to keep me warm on a chilly evening. If I will be paying bills with my laptop, I'll get my headphones so I can listen to music to make the experience even more pleasant. I'll do whatever I can think of to help set the ambience of that space so it's as comfortable as I can make it.

+ **Include the little things.** If you have space, set your favorite mug, tea bags, and a teapot or coffeemaker on a shelf or side table for an inspiring beverage break while you work or create. This helps you focus and save time. Even a pitcher of lemon water works!

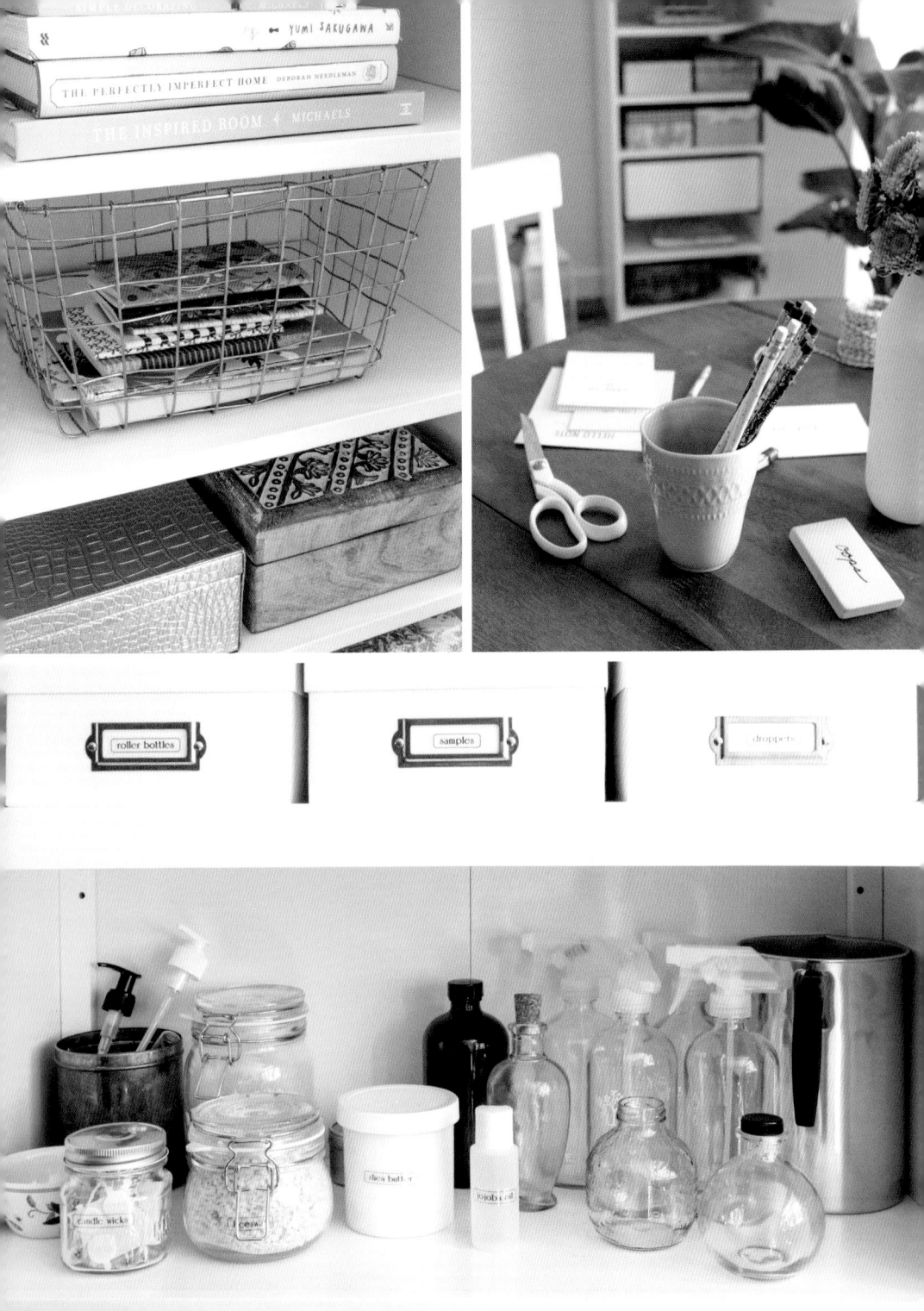

DIY | WRAPPING CENTER

If you're scrambling to hunt down gift wrapping supplies each time you have a gift to give, a simple yet all-inclusive wrapping center is just what you need. Bonus: The nature of colorful papers and supplies will add a decorative accent to any area! First, consider what type of space you have available and choose one of the following:

+ A dresser

+ An unused closet

+ A back-of-the-door rack

+ A pegboard in a hallway

+ A wall rack in a spare room

+ A shelf in a laundry room

Gather everything you need, and then get creative figuring out ways to organize your supplies.

Cards and envelopes	Postage stamps
Envelopes for gift cards	Ribbons and bows
Gift bags	Rolls of gift wrap
Fold-down boxes	Scissors and tape
Pens and pencils	Washi tape

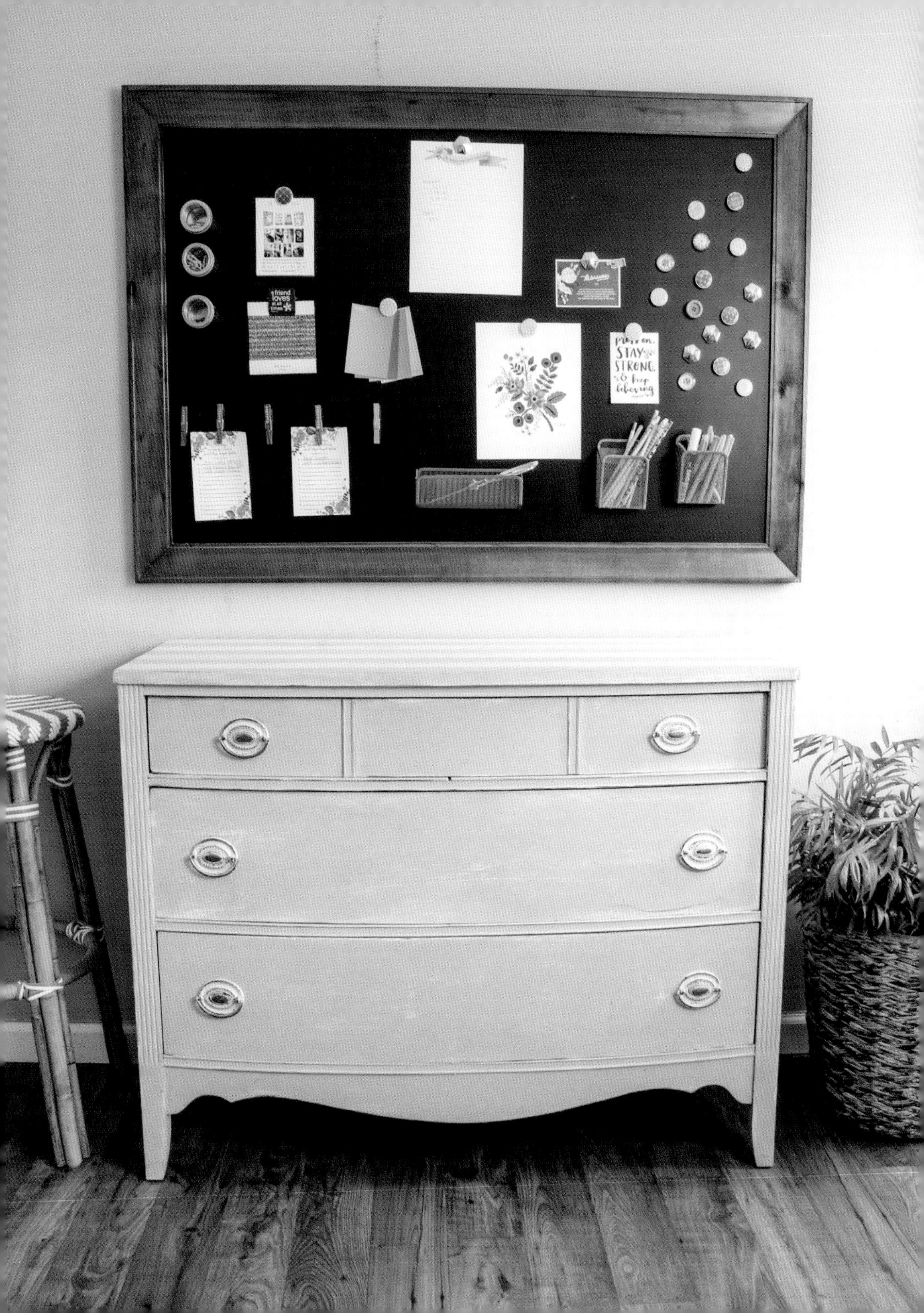
press on, STAY STRONG, & keep believing
friend loves at all times

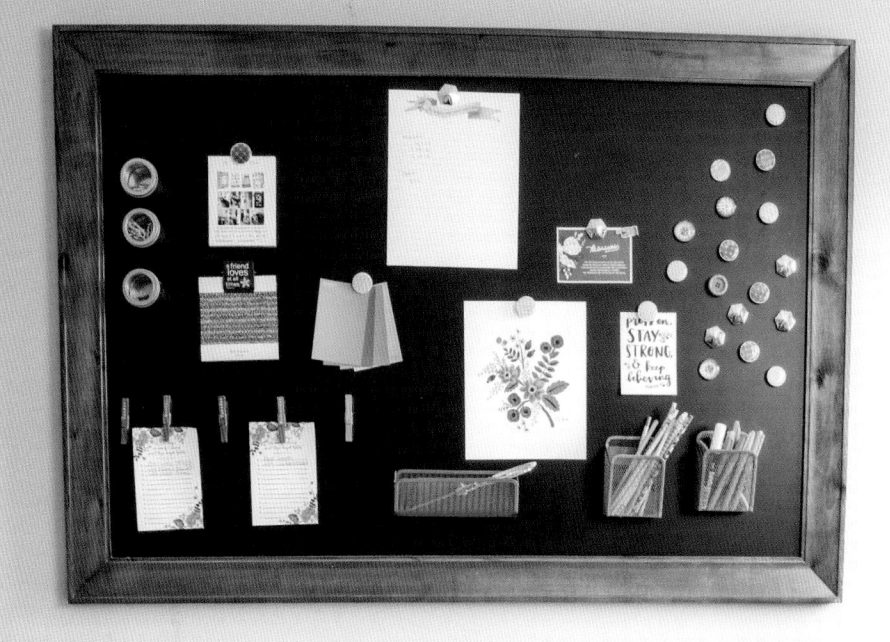

49 | FIND A HOME FOR CREATIVE SUPPLIES

In basically all households, crafting, hobby, study, and work stuff eventually end up scattered throughout different rooms. You can invest a lot of energy in picking up, or you can make some allowances for this fueled by a weekly quick cleanup session to return items to their original home.

1. If you don't have a designated room for crafts, a small basket, under-the-bed boxes, or even a secretary desk can provide space for your favorite craft or hobby.

2. Shallow drawers for crafts make it easier to keep things organized, especially small items that can easily get lost.

3. Pegboards, wall shelves, and hanging shoe organizers can maximize your vertical craft space.

4. Use labels wherever helpful to organize crafts. If you invest in a label maker, it might come in handy throughout your house!

5. Make a list of the types of activities you would like your family to be able to enjoy at home. Focus on having less random stuff, and provide more intentional opportunities to create and learn new skills through activities (such as building things, dress-up, role-playing, reading, drawing, painting, playing music or board games, cooking, doing outside exploration, etc.) to help kids (big and small) as well as grown-ups explore and develop their own talent.

6. When in doubt, invest in bookcases that offer plenty of storage space.

Conclusion

50 | EMBRACE A MIND-SET OF SIMPLICITY

If you've made it through this book, it's time to celebrate your progress. You may not have fully decluttered or organized everything in your entire home, but that's okay. Organizing is an ongoing process of simplifying your steps, creating order for the essentials, and raising your quality of living. Celebrate that you are now on a new path! With each step, you'll be developing a more fine-tuned perspective on simplicity.

As you look at your home through the lens of how *less will eventually be more*, you can more easily determine what changes *you* want to make in your home. Rather than spending time coming up with more ways to organize things you don't need, you'll more easily recognize when it's time to simply let those things go. Growing clutter and daily disorder will no longer have to be stumbling blocks.

Instead of feeling out of control and frustrated by the state of your home, you'll experience more joy in creating order. Simplicity will bring you freedom. Freedom offers you time, energy, and money to spend on what matters most to you. Organizing and housework shouldn't consume your life. Your home should be organized so that you can more fully live.

By wisdom a house is built,
and through understanding it is established;
through knowledge its rooms are filled
with rare and beautiful treasures.

PROVERBS 24:3-4

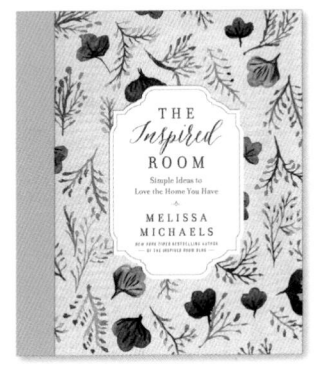

Forget the rules and discover creative ways to personalize your spaces and express your style. Create a home inspired by the people, beauty, and life you love.

Melissa invites you to experience the peace and joy that come from a well-balanced life that nurtures your home and soul throughout the year. *A Lovely Life* offers you tangible ways to make every day a better one.

Melissa wants to show you how to make small, simple changes to strengthen the connection between your home and body—your two dwellings—so you can live a healthier life filled with greater wholeness and happiness.

Is clutter taking over your home and life? Melissa gives you encouragement and practical advice to help you create a place for all the things you love.

You can love your home again when Melissa shows you how to decorate and style your rooms with ease. Dare to see your surroundings with new eyes.

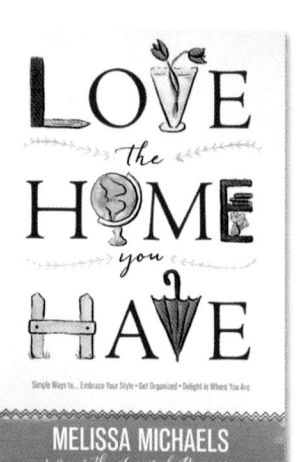

Explore simple ways to improve your well-being every day. Each month, you will be inspired to set a plan of action using the calendar pages, reflect daily on the special moments you are grateful for, and journal your thoughts using guided prompts.

Praise for *Simple Decorating*

"This book is brimming with decorating advice and inspiration you will want to test-drive in your own home after reading just the first few pages. Melissa helped me hone the style that works best for my family and lifestyle, and she shared so many real-life tips for decorating our home!"

— LIZ FOUREZ, founder of LoveGrowsWild.com, author of *A Touch of Farmhouse Charm*

"Sometimes even the most creative people get stuck when it comes to decorating their own home. Melissa is full of simple, easy-to-execute ideas that will get those decorating wheels turning! Her words motivate and nurture, and you'll want to come back to them again and again as you tweak, collect, and arrange your way through the process of making a home you love."

— MARIAN PARSONS, *Miss Mustard Seed* (blog)

What People Are Saying About *Love the Home You Have* and *The Inspired Room*

"Melissa shares how to be content and happy in our home, inspiring our home with the things we love and the people we cherish."

— ANN VOSKAMP, *New York Times* bestselling author of *One Thousand Gifts*

"Melissa Michaels' book *The Inspired Room* is full of smart, practical advice and packed with inspiration to spare. The photos are gorgeous and accompanied by helpful tips and details, and the writing lifts you up and makes you excited to dive into home decor headfirst!"

— SHERRY PETERSIK, *New York Times* bestselling author of *Young House Love*

"Melissa Michaels, how did you get into my every house-obsessed thought?"

— JILL WAAGE, executive editor, *Better Homes and Gardens* Brand

"I just love Melissa's approach to decorating to give yourself time to let the process of decorating happen in your home. Give yourself grace as well and enjoy the process."

— RACHEL DOWD, *Sweet and Simple Home* (YouTube)

"The ideas and tips Melissa shares can be done by anyone, in any decorating style, and even on the tiniest of budgets."

— DIANE HENKLER, *In My Own Style* (blog)

"Melissa is warm, down-to-earth, and exactly the kind of friend you want to come beside you to help turn your house into a home you can love and use to love others."

— MARY CARVER, author of *Choose Joy*

"Melissa offers the cure to comparison every woman needs: contentment. She'll inspire you to have a home that's not only lovely but also a true reflection of what matters most to you."

— HOLLEY GERTH, author of *You're Already Amazing*